"SHOW ME THE WHALE TEETH!"

If you were a native of the Fiji islands, you might have screamed this while trading goods with islanders across the South Pacific. Well before cash, there was a long line of monetary units used around the world. Some other less popular forms of currency have included:

- Sheep, horses, and oxen—animals were probably the original currency, used thousands of years ago by native tribes, including the Zulus and Kaffirs of Africa and American Indians.
- Ax heads—Australia's aborigines used ax heads as cash, trading them for animal products and foodstuffs with tribes hundreds of miles away.
- Tobacco—right here in the good ol' U.S.A., the early colonists swapped bundles of tobacco leaves for vital supplies from Europe.

The Pocket Professor: Everything You Need to Know About Economics explains how and why money works and how it shapes popular culture, and traces the evolution of economic theory throughout the ages. Remember, as long as you understand how today's money games are played, you'll have an edge over the sharks after your "whale teeth."

THE POCKET
PROFESSOR

ECONOMICS

THE POCKET PROFESSOR

EVERYTHING YOU NEED TO KNOW ABOUT ECONOMICS

DAVID J. FIKE, PH.D.,
AND
GREGG STEBBEN

SERIES EDITOR: DENIS BOYLES

POCKET BOOKS
New York   London   Toronto   Sydney   Singapore

The authors are grateful to American Institute for Economic Research, Great Barrington, MA 01230-1000, for permission to reproduce the following charts, which appear in the *AIER Chart Book*.

- Purchasing Power of the Dollar, page 70
- Purchasing Power of Gold, page 71
- Federal Transfer Payments by Category as Percentages of GDP, page 97
- The Median Income of Families, page 114

An *Original* Publication of POCKET BOOKS

POCKET BOOKS, a division of Simon & Schuster Inc.
1230 Avenue of the Americas, New York, NY 10020

ISBN: 0-671-53491-2

First Pocket Books trade paperback printing November 1999

10   9   8   7   6   5   4   3   2   1

Book design by Helene Wald Berinsky
Cover design by Tom McKeveny

Printed in the U.S.A.

RRDH/✕

For Sylvia

ACKNOWLEDGMENTS

I want to acknowledge the support of Holy Names College, where I am dean of faculty and have taught economics since 1992. In particular, I want to acknowledge my students; if there is anything you find useful (or humorous) in this book, it is their questioning and storytelling that is likely responsible. Furthermore, I want to acknowledge Sarah Barry Fike, my mother, who defends me (and all her sons) against all criticism (most economic writing comes with a standard "all errors are the responsibility of the author" disclaimer, but if you want to quarrel with *this* author, you gotta take it up with his mother); Thomas Lyle Fike, my father, who learned a valuable truth from his own father and then taught it to me: "It doesn't matter how much money you make—you will always spend 110% of it"; David, Valeria, and Alexandra, my children, who smile (while rolling their eyes) when I give my dinnertime lectures on economics and the other great mysteries of life; and Sylvia, my spouse, who I love *à la lune* and who inspires and encourages her "economist poet."

—David J. Fike, Ph.D.

Contents

THE POCKET PROFESSOR

EVERYTHING YOU NEED TO KNOW ABOUT ECONOMICS

ECONOMICS

It's called the "dismal science." Newspapers can't write about it because nobody wants to read about it. You can't talk about it on TV, because nobody who works in TV is smart enough to understand it. In fact, economics may never strike you as particularly interesting until that moment you wake up at 4 A.M. asking yourself this big question:

HEY, WHERE HAS ALL MY MONEY GONE?

We'll start this book by answering your late-night question with two more questions: "Where did you spend it?" and "Why did you spend it there?"

These two worthwhile questions drop us right into the heart of economics. (For the sake of conversation, in answering these two additional questions we'll assume you live in a capitalistic system where you can spend your money where you wish.)

If you're like most, you spent it on rent, food, the car payment, and shoes for the kids. Or maybe you spent it on wine and men or women and song. But isn't it nice to know that no matter how you spent it, it was all a matter of choice?

An economics professor might describe economics as "the study of the behavior of human beings in producing, distributing, and consuming material goods and services in a world of scarce resources."*

---

* In fact, we know of at least two economics professors who define economics exactly this way. We know it because we stole this definition from their book. Their names are Campbell R. McConnell and Stanley L. Brue and they wrote a textbook called *Economics: Principles, Problems, and Policies.*

Or, if you wanted to be a wise guy, like economist Jacob Viner, you'd say, "Economics is what economists do."*

Or, if you were an economist and you just wanted to make sense, you might say, as Alfred Marshall, the Cambridge economist from the turn of the twentieth century, said, "Economics is merely the study of mankind in the ordinary business of life." And John Kenneth Galbraith, the noted Harvard economist, said, "Economics is about what we earn and what we can get for it."

Duh.

But what about the rest of us? How can we make sense of this "producing, distributing, and consuming . . . in a world of scarce resources" bizness?

Let's start by breaking it down into smaller parts—and when we say *parts,* we do mean parts. Like auto parts. Computer parts. Bicycle parts. Blender parts. Chicken parts.

And for the sake of this conversation, let's rename all these parts. Let's call them *stuff.*

"YOU CALL THIS A SCIENCE?"

Now, here's a question that strikes true terror in the hearts of many economists: "Daddy [Mommy], what do you do all day?" This time, we really like the way McConnell and Brue tackle the question:

> The economist ascertains and gathers facts relevant to a specific economic problem. . . . This task is sometimes called descriptive or empirical economics. The economist also states economic principles, that is, generalizes about the way individuals and institutions actually behave. Deriving principles is called economic theory or economic analysis . . . [but] economists are as likely to move from theory to facts in studying economic behavior as they are to move from facts to theory. Stated more formally, economists use both deductive and inductive methods. Induction distills or creates principles from facts. Here an accumulation of facts is arranged systematically and analyzed to permit the derivation of a generalization or principle . . . [but] generalizations may also be created

---

* As you can see, Viner had a lot better sense of humor about his job than McConnell and Brue do.

through deduction or the hypothetical method. Here economists draw upon casual observation, insight, logic, or intuition to frame a tentative, untested principle called an hypothesis. For example, they may conjecture, on the basis of "armchair logic," that it is rational for consumers to buy more of a product when its price falls.*

In other words, Daddy or Mommy makes a living by playing "let's pretend."

THE STUFF OF WHICH ECONOMIC DREAMS ARE MADE

Remember our boring old definition of economics? "... the study of the behavior of human beings in producing, distributing, and consuming material goods and services in a world of scarce resources." How about if we take it apart and examine it piece by piece:

... the study of the behavior of human beings ...
Well, we figure this first one is pretty self-explanatory. So let's try the next part:

... producing, distributing and consuming ...
Now, this seems straightforward. As human beings, we make things (produce) and bring them to other human beings (distribute), who use the things we made (consume). But, actually, it gets a little more complicated. What are these things that we produce, distribute, and consume? Well, the definition calls them:

... material goods and ...
You know that new-and-improved digital power widget you've been dying to get? Even when there's nothing wrong with the old manual analog widget you've already got?
Well, that new power widget is stuff.
And where does that new power widget come from?
It comes from stuff, a.k.a. parts.

---

* Campbell R. McConnell, Stanley L. Brue, *Economics, thirteenth edition* (McGraw-Hill, 1996), #3.

And where did that stuff—the parts, come from?

More stuff.

If you take your brand-new widget apart, you'll find it is jam-packed with stuff. And some of that stuff is made up of other stuff. More parts.

Smaller and smaller gets the stuff. Little bitty parts put together to make slightly bigger parts, put together to make slightly bigger parts, put together to make—well, you get the idea.

Go into the garage or the kitchen or your kid's room and pick something up. Anything. Just pick up a piece of stuff.

Now, look at it closely.

That stuff is made of stuff.

Stuff is easy to see if you pick up the toaster or the hand drill or the little one's bright yellow computer mouse. There's all kinds of stuff—screws and nuts and hinges and joints and plugs—all assembled in such a way so as to make something useful like a toaster or a hand drill or a yellow computer mouse.

The concept is slightly harder to see if you pick up a towel or a washcloth or a pillowcase. But look closely. What is that piece of fabric made of? True, there are no screws or bolts or nifty fastening devices (only lowly thread) holding it all together, but if you look closely you can see that your favorite grimy weekend T-shirt is merely the woven sum of its threaded parts. Or stuff. All stuff comes from stuff.

Stuff has to start somewhere. And that somewhere is usually somewhere in the ground. Metal gets mined, fruits and vegetables get farmed, and so on. This is the stuff economists call material goods.

The other kinds of things we produce, distribute, and consume are called

... services ...

In other words, not all stuff is stuff you can touch. In fact, more and more and more of it in the modern economy is like what most of us do at our jobs all day. When we're producing, we're talking, typing, meeting, computing, consulting, and thinking, but we're not producing the way a farmer or a miner or a factory worker does. We are doing what economists call providing services.

So, stuff is everywhere. Stuff can be things you can touch (material goods) and stuff can be things you can't touch (services). Got it?

So far so good. Economics is the study of how we make and use stuff. So, what's this last little part of the definition?

... in a world of scarce resources ...

Well, this last little phrase is a big deal. In fact, scarcity is the key to studying economics. So what is it?

Well, basically it means that you can never get everything you want.

If you are really poor—say, unable to feed your children three squares a day—you don't need an economist to tell you about scarcity. But according to economists, scarcity affects you even if you're wealthy.

How come? Because even the wealthy never have everything they want. For example, you might say, "I'll never be able to get one of those" when you think about getting a Porsche like your boss's. Ironically, if Porsches like your boss's grew on trees and everyone had one, you'd probably want a Ferrari instead.

And Martha Stewart, who is rich and famous precisely because she has led us all to believe that she has everything she could possibly want, was once heard to say, "I have a beautiful weekend house in the Hamptons, but it is not, as it turns out, my summer dream house. It doesn't have the view of the ocean that I absolutely want. It doesn't have the rustic wood floors that I absolutely crave. It doesn't have a little dock to which I can tie my little rowboat. And it doesn't have the shallow water of a quiet lagoon where I can pick my plants." So you can see that even when you are Martha Stewart and you have everything you could possibly want, there is always something more to want.

Of course, getting that "something different" produced so Martha can consume it takes stuff (also known to economists as resources). And stuff used to make other stuff, like everything else, is scarce. This is true about stuff you can touch, like the wood needed to produce Martha's rustic floors or her little rowboat. It is also true about stuff you can't touch, like the services Martha's gardener might provide.

Scarcity, as you can see, is that which makes it all interesting.

THE SEVEN DIRTY WORDS OF ECONOMICS

Psst!

Hey, you!

Wanna sound like an economist?

First, you've gotta memorize their seven-word vocabulary:

1. **Supply:** How much of a particular stuff is there?
2. **Demand:** How much of that particular stuff do you want?
3. **Scarcity:** There's never enough of the good stuff to go around.
4. **Equilibrium:** What you call it when there's exactly enough good stuff for everyone who wants it . . . and is willing to pay the price for it. (This never really happens, by the way.)
5. **Marginal:** . . . : In economics, *marginal* is everywhere you look. There's marginal cost, marginal revenue, marginal input, marginal output, marginal loss, marginal profit, marginal satisfaction, and—we just *love* this one—marginal thinking. In every case, *marginal* means the same thing: how much cost/revenue/input/output/loss/profit/satisfaction/thinking will be gained or lost by adding or subtracting one unit of whatever it is we're talking about. For instance, if you own a business that makes Fuzzy-Wuzzys and you want to know if it would be worth adding one more employee on the manufacturing line, you would partake in a little marginal analysis. You would compare what it costs to employ that person (including benefits and all other related costs) to what you would gain by adding him or her. You'd ask yourself, "How much more product would that employee produce? For how much could I sell that additional product?" Once you'd answered these questions, you would compare the cost of hiring the new employee with how much you would make by having him or her there. If it looks like you'll make money on the deal, hire away. If it looks like you'll lose money or just break even, stop dreaming and get back to work—but take a minute to appreciate the fact that if you didn't understand how to evaluate the marginal costs and marginal benefits of hiring someone new, the odds that you would have made the right decision for your business would have been, well, marginal.
6. **Aggregate:** The great-granddaddy of *marginal.* For every aspect of economics that can be viewed from a marginal point of view, there is an aggregate point of view as well. Whereas the marginal perspective is one in which you look at the addition or subtraction of one more unit, in aggregate thinking you are always looking at the total of all the elements involved. Therefore, in the example above in which you consider hiring another employee, the marginal perspective is one in which you consider the costs and benefits of the addition of one more. In the aggregate perspective you consider all your employees, all your costs, all the production, and all the revenue.

7. **Competition:** The unspoken and unwritten law that (in theory) keeps all businesses honest. If my factory starts producing low-quality Fuzzy-Wuzzys (or Fuzzys that are too expensive), for instance, it's a sure bet that someone else will open a factory and produce a better Fuzzy (or the same Fuzzy for a cheaper price). Fear of that alone keeps me motivated to strive for the highest possible quality at the lowest price.

For 2,800 other dirty words (and theories, institutions and schools of thought) of economics, see *The MIT Dictionary of Modern Economics* (edited by David W. Pearce), an authoritative reference on economic terminology, nomenclature, and other important stuff.

DOGGED ECONOMICS

No one can teach you about scarcity quicker than the family dog.

Try this test at home: Bring all of your dog's favorite toys and bones together and heap them in a pile in the middle of the living-room floor. If your dog is like most, he'll have a hard time deciding which he'd rather chew on, so he'll pick one up, chew, drop it, then pick up another.

Now, the experiment begins: It's your turn to pick a favorite plaything.

Notice that once you grab a toy, the dog immediately wants it, too. Drop that toy and grab another, and he'll instantly want your new toy of choice. Give him that toy so you can grab yet another, and he'll be happy only when he has the one that is currently in your hand.

Scarcity. Always wanting that which we cannot have. You do it. We do it. Even simple Rover does it.

TRACING THE ROOTS OF STUFF

As you now know, before the stuff we buy at the store becomes that kind of stuff, it is most often some other kind of stuff that's found in, on, or around the ground.

To get it from the ground to the store, someone had to gather it all up. Someone else had to invest in the land from which it was taken. Someone else had to invent the machinery to get the stuff out of the earth, and someone else had to provide a truck or a train or a plane or a car by which it could be moved from the earth where it was found to the factory where it was made into parts. Someone else had to build the factory. Someone else had to dig in the earth for the fuel that it took to dig for the stuff and to move the stuff to somewhere else and to make the truck or train or plane or car in which it moved—not to mention digging for the fuel to make the factory run so the stuff could be turned into different stuff.

Speaking of fuel, some of the stuff that is removed from the earth is fuel for you and us. Food. It follows the same process described above, however. And we burn that fuel just like a truck burns diesel fuel.

We, the workers, are like trucks in another way, too. We use fuel to provide work. You eat breakfast. You go to your office; you do your job. Until lunchtime, when you have more fuel so you can provide more work.

But let's look at stuff in a different light.

For instance, take the motor in your new power widget. The only reason it's a power widget motor instead of an electric hairbrush motor is that enough people said they wanted power widgets and no one said he or she wanted an electric hairbrush. So the owner of the land and the owner of the factory and the owner of the train or plane or car all came to the conclusion that it'd be wise to forget about electric hairbrushes and instead devote their resources to producing the stuff of which power widgets are made.

When most people get up in the morning and go to work, they do what they do because the boss or the owner tells them to do it. If the boss says to make electric hairbrushes, they do it. If the boss says to make battery-powered pocket knives, they do that instead.

The boss, on the other hand, marches to the beat of a different drummer. For instance, he or she decides to make motor-driven widgets instead of hairbrushes.

Why?

Because he or she has determined that the market—that's you and me and everyone else on the globe with a dollar (or the equivalent) in their pocket—values those widgets more than it would value those hairbrushes. (Okay, we're fudging a bit here. It's not so much that we value one over the other—instead, the boss has weighed costs against revenues and determined that he or she can make more money making widgets than making hairbrushes even though electric hairbrushes might actually cost more and therefore be considered more valuable.)

Regardless of what the boss decides, however, he or she has to choose one course of action over the other . . . and we feel confident in saying we're sure the boss will do what provides him or her with the greatest gain. In other words, it's simply an economic decision.

Just as the boss will try to make economic decisions that maximize the benefits of his or her limited resources, you may find yourself in the same position.

If company A offers to pay you $8 per hour for your time and company B offers to pay you $10 per hour, which job will you take? It's a question with an easy answer. It's an economic decision. All things being equal, you'll take the job that pays you more.

Ahhh . . . but what if company B will make you work lifting heavy boxes all day, whereas company A will ask you to just sit in a chair and answer the phone?

The choice is not as clear . . . yet it is still an economic decision. Some people enjoy physical exertion and would therefore be happy to work a little harder to make a little more money. Others would prefer to sit. Therefore, *they* would be happy to make a little less money for a less physically taxing job.

This is an oversimplification, of course. Garbage collectors make thousands and movie stars make millions—yet the same principle applies.

After all, the relative number of job opportunities available to garbage collectors and the average salary of all garbage collectors across the board is remarkably different from the opportunities available to actors (if you don't count the work they do as waiters—we're betting only 3% to 5% of all men and women in this country who call themselves actors actually get acting work that pays). Compare the percentage of garbage collectors who are able to find work to the percentage of actors who are able to find work, then compare the number of garbage collectors who are able to earn a living wage to the number of actors who are able to earn a living wage, and you realize something: If being a successful actor were as easy as being a successful garbage collector, we'd all be leading an actor's life.

But being an actor comes with no guarantees, and a career as a garbage collector offers significantly more job security.

So how did all those garbage collectors go about choosing their careers?

Easy. It was all a matter of economics.

VEGETARIAN ECONOMICS

So you think economics is dry?

At least when we talk about *micro* and *macro*, you know that at some point we're going to end up talking about money. When vegetarians talk about *micro* and *macro*, what they're really talking about is buckwheat and brown rice and yogurt with *Lactobacillus acidophilus*.

In honor of our vegetarian friends, we'll think of the economy as a frog.

If you dissect the frog (a decidedly nonvegetarian thing to do, so we must remind you that we are speaking hypothetically here and ask that you not try this at home), you see that it is made up of parts—remember that word?—or stuff. It has legs and eyes and a heart. And if you use a microscope to look at its parts even closer, you can see that its parts are made up of parts. This is analogous to the study of microeconomics.

An economist who studies microeconomics might study a particular industry, a particular company, or even a particular type of household to understand how it fits into the economy at large, just as a high school biology student studies the frog's organs in an attempt to understand how they work together to build one fully functional frog.

Those who are squeamish, on the other hand, will be delighted to know that macroeconomics is the study of the whole frog. In fact, macroeconomists are a bit like high school students who choose to forgo the dissection experience in lieu of hiding their frogs in their teacher's desk. They don't want to study parts; they want to know what'll happen when the teacher opens the drawer.

THE FROG PRINC(IPLE)

To stick with our frog analogy here, just as kids love to predict when a frog will jump—and how high—macroeconomists are often trying to predict when interest rates will do the same thing.

BETTY CROCKER ECONOMICS

Like bakers who ply their craft with flour, sugar, an eggbeater and a well-oiled pan, economists, too, have a standard set of tools:

- **Facts:** Stuff that is known and quantifiable.
- **Principles:** Theories or generalizations about widely recognized and accepted economic behaviors. For instance, since we have an economic system that makes money scarce and valuable, we can generalize about most people and say that there is a point at which everyone will bend over to pick up a stray coin or bill off the street. For some, all it takes is a penny. For others, it might take a dollar. For a few, it might take a hundred. But the principle applies in every case.
- **Policies:** Unlike the baker, however, who will bake you a cake like nobody can, economists try to cook up good policy. Policies are the rules that govern individual or group or business behavior. For instance, a company might be involved in a business practice that results in a form of pollution. Without some form of governmental policy in place to regulate, restrict or even outlaw that practice, some businesses would continue to pollute without giving it a second thought. On the other hand, when the government institutes a policy that requires the business to pay certain fees or fines that rapidly increase as the amount of pollution increases, suddenly the business has an economic incentive to keep its pollution to a minimum.

> Just add water: The subtitle of the book *The Instant Economist* by John Charles Pool and Ross M. LaRoe is *All the Basic Principles of Economics in One Hundred Pages of Plain Talk.* This easy-reader is long on concepts and short on detail, but as promised, it will have you looking at the world in economic terms in just one sitting.

In fact, interest-rate behavior is typical of the topics studied by macroeconomists, who don't want to look at parts (individual banks or your particular mortgage) but would rather examine the whole scene involving all the banks, borrowers, brokerage houses, U.S. Department of the Treasury, and the Federal Reserve System.

Macroeconomists also look at the behavior of overall prices. Not the increase in the price of a particular product like your yellow computer mouse, but the increase in prices in general—otherwise known as inflation. They also look at the behavior of overall employment

> **WHAT YOU MIGHT EXPECT TO LEARN FROM THIS BOOK . . .**
> . . . if it were a two-semester college course by Woody Allen . . .
>
> Economic Theory: A systematic application and critical evaluation of the basic analytic concepts of economic theory with an emphasis on money and why it's good. Fixed coefficient production functions, cost and supply curves, and nonconvexity comprise the first semester, with the second semester concentrating on spending, making change, and keeping a neat wallet. The Federal Reserve System is analyzed, and advance students are coached in the proper method of filling out a deposit slip. Other topics include: Inflation and Depression—how to dress for each—loans, interest, welching.
>
> —WOODY ALLEN, IN HIS BOOK *GETTING EVEN*

conditions—not whether you or your neighbor can get a job, but whether lots of people are tending to get jobs, so that overall, the percentage of unemployed people is going up or going down.

In reality, economics is a rather simple science . . . as far as sciences go.

After all, isn't it a lot easier to understand how people will behave—as individuals or in large numbers or as corporations or governments or nations—in a given situation than it is to understand the behavior of atoms or molecules or fish or cells or the weather? When it comes to human beings, after all, you are a member of the sampling pool.

Therefore, the same advice that Obi-Wan Kenobi offered Luke Skywalker in the original *Star Wars* movie—"Luke! Let the force be with you!"—will benefit you in your study of economics. The answers are all within you.

On the other hand, applying the abstract to the specific in economics can sometimes get tricky—so let's take a look at the rules of the game:

THE FIVE LAWS OF ECONOMICS
THE THEORIES BEHIND THE LAWS
Law #1: The Law of Demand
The more of it there is to go around, the less people are willing to pay for it; conversely, the less of it there is to go around, the more people are willing to pay for it.

Let's take the case of air and diamonds.

Air is one of the most plentiful things in the world and diamonds are one of the rarest.

According to the law of demand, that means most people aren't willing to pay much for air (since it's so accessible) but they understand that if they want to buy a diamond, they're going to have to pay a lot (since diamonds are so scarce).

If we used air instead of diamonds to express our love, it would

---

MAYBE OBI HEARD IT FROM THE ANCIENT GREEKS?

Frequently when one studies economics in the abstract, it actually seems like pretty easy stuff.

No wonder. As we've said before, economics is all about you.

If you want to talk about microeconomics, then it's got to be about you. After all, you are the parts. You own the household; you work at the company; you are a member of the industry. So even if it isn't you they're talking about on the news when they talk about the economy, at least they're talking about someone you know—your next-door neighbor, your coworker, your boss, the owner of your company.

Sometimes, though, the news of the economy is about bigger things, like the entire country (you and all your neighbors).

As you'll see as you read on, the same economic principles that apply to the parts (you and your immediate neighbors) also apply to the whole (you and all those of your country or all your fellow human beings).

It's just that sometimes economists give these principles different names. But don't let their fancy lingo throw you—after all, the word *economics* is from the ancient Greek. And when you translate *economics* back to the mother tongue, it becomes nothing more complicated than the "art of household management."

Moreover, *micro* comes from the Greek word for "small," as in "your neighbor is small in comparison to the whole country." And *macro* comes from the Greek word for "big," as in "it's a big country—I wouldn't want to paint it."

A few thousand years later, economists are still trying to explain what they do. One who does a good job of it is James Eggert, in his book *What Is Economics?*

be a gesture so cheap and common it would be insulting. It would almost seem to imply "Honey, I love you as much as this cup of air I just went outside to get, and you know, if I hadn't scooped up this particular cup of air I could have scooped up any cup of air because hey, it's just air. There's nothing special about it."

True love is a priceless, rare, and uncommon thing; therefore, we use the diamond, another rare and uncommon thing, as a symbol for expressing it.

When we give our love a diamond, we want to say, "I chose this diamond because it is unique and there is no other diamond like it in the world—just as with my love for you, there is no other love like it in the world."

Of course, there's another way to express the same law, and it goes like this: The more you want it, the more you have to pay for it, and the less you want it, the less you have to pay for it.

Imagine, for example, that clean air became inaccessible. Suddenly, you'd want clean air very badly. And we bet you'd be willing to pay for it.

Law #2: The Law of Supply

The more people are willing to pay for something, the more of it other people are going to try to produce; the less people are willing to pay for something, the less of it other people are going to try to produce.

In other words, if people are willing to pay a lot for diamonds, other people will find a way to supply them. Same thing with air.

In fact, since clear air in some cities like Los Angeles, Toronto, and Tokyo can be hard to find, people really are willing to pay for it. And, not surprisingly, other people are willing to supply it via oxygen bars, where you can go if you need to catch a breath of fresh air.

Law #3: The Law of Elasticity

If you're flexible, you pay less, and if you're inflexible, you pay more.

For some people, a sneaker is a sneaker is a sneaker. For others, only a Nike will do.

If you think a sneaker is a sneaker is a sneaker, then you'll go to

Kmart or Wal-Mart or some such discount store and buy the cheapest tennis shoe you can find. Your demand for any particular brand or style of sneaker is elastic. You're flexible. You're willing to bend. On the other hand, if you believe only a Nike will do, you are inelastic. Inflexible. You're not willing to give in at all. If you have to drive 100 miles to get Nikes, you do it. If the Reeboks are on sale and half the price of the Nikes you normally get, you're still going to buy the Nikes.

Another example: for some people, rock 'n' roll is rock 'n' roll. But if you've got a hankering to hear Mick Jagger sing "Satisfaction," then no Yoko Ono or Garth Brooks or Muzak version of "Satisfaction" will satisfy you. You are completely and utterly inflexible. Utterly and completely inelastic—only the Rolling Stones will do.

This is an important concept in economics. It helps explain why brand-name products (and Rolling Stones concert tickets) are so expensive.

Law #4: The Law of Self-Interest
Given a choice, you will always do what is best for you.

One of your authors is a notorious cheapskate. To him, the only standard by which a banking institution should be judged is by the amount it charges in fees. And any fee over a penny is, in his estimation, too much. In other words, he doesn't want to pay a cent to do his banking.

In fact, your author will do almost anything to avoid paying a banking fee. If that means he cannot ever go inside the bank to do his banking, lest they levy a fee, he will do all his banking online or at an ATM. If it means he has to drive 10 minutes out of his way to one of his own bank's free ATMs to withdraw cash once in a while, he'll do it.

This particular author's wife, on the other hand, has a different standard by which she judges the value of a bank. She likes to go inside the bank, chat with the tellers, have a cup of coffee, read the bank's free literature, and generally bask in the experience. She is a commercial artist by training and therefore will keep her money only in a bank that (1) looks nice from the outside, (2) feels nice on the inside, (3) has pleasant employees who are ready to chat, and (4) provides coffee and something to read. (Oh, and the something to read must be well written and attractively designed—otherwise, what's the point?) She concedes, however, that she is asking for her bank to provide her with a lot . . . so she is perfectly happy paying a small monthly fee for this pleasant banking experience. Needless to say, your author and his wife keep their money in different banking institutions. Your author has found a bank that serves his best interest—that is, he doesn't have to pay to bank there, but they won't let him walk through the door and talk to a human being without charging him for it, and he has to drive out of his way once in a while to get money from an ATM for free. To him, it's worth it. If he plays by the rules, he gets the free checking he so loves. His wife, on the other hand, has found an attractive bank that looks good on the outside, feels good on the inside, hires only the most pleasant bank tellers, serves free coffee, and puts a lot of care into the writing and design of its brochures. All of these added amenities contribute to the satisfaction of what is important to her—her self-interest—and she's perfectly happy to pay for it every month.

The law of self-interest is tricky because it requires you to concede that what is best for you may not be best for someone else. Instead, you get to choose what is best for you, and everyone else gets to choose what is best for themselves.

Law #5: The Law of Economic Reality
No matter what the situation, some combination of laws 1 through 4 will apply.

WHERE THE RUBBER MEETS THE ROAD
Hey! C'mon! Let's take those five laws of economics out on the windy, curvy track called "your life" and put them to the test:

Let's say you're the office manager for the local branch of American Widget. The economy's gone bad and the company's closing your office. You're out of work for the first time in your life.

Meanwhile, the economic picture in your town is looking so bleak that the only work you can find at all is as a low-paid bicycle messenger or short-order cook.

Bummer.

So what should you do?

Well, let's apply laws 1 through 5:

Law #1A: The Law of Demand

Suddenly, you remember that when you accepted your last job, the economy had been booming and there were more jobs than people to take them.

Back then, a really good office manager such as you was almost impossible to find. When American Widget offered you the job, you knew you had the company over the barrel: If the company didn't hire you, it'd have to hire some kid who was currently working as a—gulp!—bicycle messenger or short-order cook. There was no one else around. So you really played hard to get—you made American Widget pay you twice your previous salary and you demanded a big office with a view, a parking space with your name on it, and your own secretary, and you even held out for the right to eat in the executive dining room with all the other big cheeses.

Boy, those were the days!

Now, the complete opposite is true. There are lots of good office managers looking for work . . . and you know what that means: The more of it there is to go around, the less people are willing to pay for it; conversely, the less of it there is to go around, the more people are willing to pay for it.

In this case, the people are prospective employers. And they ain't willin' to pay you much . . . because they know that they don't have to. So you're going to have to pay instead—by taking a lower-paying job.

Law #1B: The Law of Demand (An Alternative Perspective)

Let's look at your situation from a prospective employer's perspective.

From his or her point of view, there are lots of "yous"—that is, lots of other unemployed office managers out there who are looking for work—and, unfortunately, there aren't enough jobs for all of them. So guess what? The supply of workers is high and demand for them is low—so the employer knows that he or she is not going to have to pay as much to hire you as would have been necessary when demand for good employees was high and the supply was low. Back then, people like you could get away with demanding things like window offices and exclusive dining privileges. So where you were once thrilled to be on the receiving end of the law of demand because you knew the more your employer wanted you the more he/she had to pay, now you begrudgingly appreciate the corollary of the law, which states that the less an employer wants you, the less he/she has to pay to get you.

Law #2: The Law of Supply

As you'll recall, the law of supply says that the more people are willing to pay for something, the more of it other people are going to try to produce, and the less people are willing to pay for something, the less of it other people are going to try to produce.

It's funny how you have inadvertently become a walking example of this.

Since employers are currently willing to pay less for a good office manager than they were in the past, you are less willing to serve in the job. The problem is, from your perspective, there aren't any other comparable jobs out there for you, either. You are therefore stuck in a supply-side nightmare.

Law #3: The Law of Elasticity

Here's where things get tricky. You sure don't want to work for less money than you made at your last job, but it looks like you won't have much choice. And if that isn't bad enough, it looks like you'll have to work for a lot less money *and* like you'll have to take a lot less desirable job.

So, how flexible are you?

You'll remember that the law of elasticity says that if you're flexible, you pay less, and if you're inflexible, you pay more—but in this case we're talking about not what you pay but what you give up.

If you take a lower-paying job, you pay by giving up what you consider to be your real earning power or what you think you deserve to be paid. Taking a job as a bike messenger or short-order cook will also require you to work in a job for which you consider yourself to be far overqualified.

Again, you are paying by giving up. By accepting one of those jobs as a bicycle messenger or short-order cook (or both, if that's what it takes to make ends meet) you are giving up (lowering) your standards when it comes to the type of employment for which you consider yourself to be suited.

Law #4: The Law of Self-Interest

Now, it's decision time . . . and it's a decision that only you can make. Will you (1) go without work until the right job comes along or (2) take a job that pays less than you're accustomed to earning and for which you are also drastically overqualified?

If you are like most people, the right answer will be immediately apparent to you. Ironically, that's why this is called the law of self-interest. Just because the right answer is obviously right to you doesn't mean it's the right answer for everyone.

If you're young and unmarried, the right answer might be to take all your money out of the bank, buy a backpack, and hitchhike through Europe until the economy improves. After all, what have you got to lose?

On the other hand, you might be the parent of three and the proud owner of a large mortgage. In the face of possibly losing your home and not being able to feed your children, the apparent right answer would probably be to work days as a bicycle messenger and nights as a short-order cook, if that's what was required to take care of your family.

Law #5: The Law of Economic Reality

As the law states, no matter what the situation, some combination of laws 1 through 4 will apply—as you have just seen.

HOW TO APPLY THE FIVE LAWS OF ECONOMICS IN YOUR OWN LIFE

These laws are sort of like suntan lotion. You no longer ask, "Do I need it?" when you're in the sun. Instead, you ask, "Which one do I need?" You can choose not to use any at all, but you know you're going to fry, and you may pay for the damage for the rest of your life.

Same thing in economics. You can go through life without applying the laws of economics, but guaranteed, you're gonna get burned.

So let's try out some case studies:

The Case of the Overpriced Mazda

Chances are that if you want something, so does everyone else. And if everyone else wants it, too, then the folks who're selling it know they can raise their price.

Since you all want it so badly, you'll pay the higher price. So the sellers will raise their price again. And most people will still pay it (but a few won't). The sellers will raise again. Most will pay. The sellers will raise. A few less will pay . . . etc. Until the sellers raise the price too high and most people decide they don't want it that bad. So the sellers will lower the price. More will buy, but not enough. So the sellers will again lower the price. And even more will buy. And the sellers will lower the price. And even more will buy. Eventually, the price will be back to about where it started, if not lower.

A good example of this?

The Mazda Miata.

When this flashy little sports car was introduced in 1989, it took the auto world by storm. There was nothing else on the market like it and Mazda dealers were immediately able to sell the car for more than the sticker price.

Well, that lasted for a while. Only those who could afford the luxury of paying more than the suggested retail price could afford to have a Miata. Soon, all those who were willing to pay a premium for the car had one.

So, naturally, Mazda dealers began to sell the cars for exactly the sticker price—not a penny more, not a penny less.

Pretty soon, everyone who was willing to pay sticker price for a new Miata had one.

Now what?

Mazda dealers began to treat the Miata like any other new car on their lots—they made deals for them. Demand had dropped; therefore, so did the price.

The Case of the Freebie Cell Phone . . . or the Inverse Miata Principle

Suppose someone's got something to sell, but at the asking price, no one wants to buy.

What's the seller to do?

Lower the price until a few people buy. Then lower it again until more buy. And then lower it again until even more buy.

It may have all begun with the invention of the copy machine. Before businesses had photocopiers, they had mimeograph, or ditto, machines. The machines were horrible and messy and slow but better than nothing—and nobody knew any better.

Along came Xerox. They had invented a machine that would take a picture of whatever it was you wanted to copy, and it would print that picture on another piece of paper. And it did it really fast.

The problem was that not only was the machine really fast but it was also really expensive. So expensive, in fact, that no one was willing to pay it. The only way Xerox could get people to replace their slow and messy ditto machine with the clean and fast Xerox copier was to give the copiers away—and then charge anyone who took the machine a nickel for every copy they made.

Fast-forward to the present. Go into any electronics store in the country and they'll give you a free cell phone. But only if you sign up for a year's worth of service.

Just like Xerox, the cell phone companies know there's a lot more money to be made on your monthly bill than there is on the phone. So much money, in fact, that they can afford to give the phone away.

Want a low-tech example of the same principle at work?

Take the razor. There was a time when guys shaved with standard-size razor blades. You bought the razor of your choice and the blades of your choice and shaved to your heart's content. One size fit all. Today, you buy a fancy Schick razor or a fancy Gillette razor or a fancy whatever-else-brand-you-want razor, and you get it pretty cheap . . . but once you choose your razor, you have to buy the matching blades. Schick's blades don't fit Gillette razors. Gillette blades don't fit Wilkinson razors. Suddenly, you've become a customer for life . . . or at least for the life of your razor.

The concept at work here is called bundling. If the copy-machine salesperson, cell phone company representative, or razor company can count on you as a captive paying customer in the future, it's well worth their while to give you the copier, cell phone, or razor for free.

The Case of the Supermarket Sneakers

As you know, for at least one of your authors a sneaker is a sneaker is a sneaker.

ANOTHER PERSPECTIVE ON THE CELLULAR PHONE MARKET

Not only do you get the phone for free because they know they'll make it up on the air time, but you also get the phone for free because it's really last year's expensive model. It works like this: As long as there continues to be a flow of new and improved and high-priced phones into the market for those people who always want to be on the cutting edge of technology, there will always be a flow of left-over last year's groovy models to serve as this year's cheap (a.k.a. free) phones.

In fact, if you take a mental tally of all your friends with cell phones, you'll find they come in two types: those who always seem to have a new, better, faster phone and those who got a free phone when they first got cell service and have stuck with it for years, in spite of all the innovations that have followed. Logically, then, it's your friends who are the buyers of the latest and greatest cell phones who are funding the continuing research and development in cell-phone technology and making it possible for the rest of us to get free phones.

I buy my sneakers at Kmart. I buy them there because they only cost $5.99 a pair.

You, of course, are appalled.

You buy only those sneakers with Pete Sampras's or Michael Jordan's autograph on them. You like the way they look, and, you reason, they also make you a better athlete.

You're accustomed to laying out $150 a pair.

The point of this case study is not to prove that one of us is wrong but to find a rationale that will allow both of us to be right. After all, only you can know what sneaker will best serve your own interest, and only I can know which will serve my own interest.

Although on the surface buying a pair of sneakers may seem like a fairly innocent, inconsequential, and meaningless event in one's life, in reality the decisions you make at the shoe store (or sporting goods store or Kmart) tell economists a lot about you . . . and collectively, the shoes we buy tell economists a lot about us as a society. First of all, in many parts of the world choosing which pair of sneakers to buy is an inelastic buying decision. If you are poor you buy the cheap ones and consider yourself lucky to have a new pair of shoes at all.

In this country, however, many people are wealthy enough to be able to consider sneakers that range in price from $5.99 to the sky's the limit. And there are buyers for sneakers at every price point along the way.

If you and I were to debate our sneaker choices, you might say you like your Pete Sampras shoes because they make you feel significantly better. I, on the other hand, would reply that I once tried on a pair of Pete Sampras sneakers and I didn't think they felt much different than my "blue light" specials. Neither of us is right in this debate, by the way.

Rather, by buying your $150.00 Pete Samprases, you are saying not only that you feel better in them but also that they make you feel $144.01 better than a pair of my $5.99 sneakers would.

Well, if that's the case, I might ask, *why don't you buy the $200 Michael Jordan sneakers and feel even better yet?*

You might respond by explaining that you couldn't afford the additional $50 or that you wouldn't feel right spending that much money for a pair of sneakers—but what you'd really be saying, in economic terms, is that you don't think the Michael Jordans will make you feel $50 better than the Pete Samprases.

Ah, but is there a price you could put on the degree to which the Jordans make you feel better than the Samprases? One way to tell is to see how you respond the next time you go in to buy a pair of Samprases and see that the Jordans are on sale.

But let's get back to me and my Kmart sneakers. Because I think there's no difference between my sneakers and yours, and because price is my only buying criteria, I might scoff at you and believe you are buying those expensive shoes only for the status you think they will bestow on you.

I might be right. You might feel better because you believe people will see that trademarked symbol and admire you for choosing it. Or you might believe that you'll gain the upper hand over an opponent on the tennis court because he or she will see that status symbol and assume you are a better player than you are and give you the mental edge.

Are image, status, and a possible mental edge worth $144.01?

This is a question that only you can answer for you and that only I can answer for myself.

ECONOMIC TRUTH . . . OR CONSEQUENCES

When it comes to money and other instruments of economic significance, questions have a way of arising:

■ **Where does my money come from?**

Some money is earned with less sweat than other money, but all money is earned. Or maybe you don't remember the old Smith Barney ads for the company now called Salomon Smith Barney: "We make money the old-fashioned way . . . we earn it."

If you're like most people, then we could say the same thing about you. You go to work every day and earn your money by the sweat of your brow. (Or, if you're lucky, you were born into wealth and you're living off the interest, but then you don't need this book. You're too busy having fun in the south of France.)

Money always comes from the same place—that is, it comes in exchange for something else, and that something else must provide some sort of value to someone else who is willing to fork over some do-re-mi for it.

In short, your money comes from someone else. You must do something (or have something) that someone else values and is willing to pay for. If you work for McDonald's, you get paid to make burgers that other carnivores are willing to pay for. If you work for Salomon Smith Barney, you get paid to help other people invest their money . . . and they value your help enough to pay you for it. And if you are wealthy and live off your parents' money, then banks pay you (in the form of interest) for the right to use your money because they find value in the arrangement. It's not hard to see how it works: They borrow your money and pay you 5% for it, let's say, and then they lend it to someone else at 7%. They just made money, and so did you. Hooray! Collect that $200 as you pass Go. Ain't life grand?

■ **And why does money go so fast?**

In a word: inflation.

Of course you want (and expect) your boss to give you a raise every year. So does everyone else.

But what if the money to pay your raise comes from the newly increased price of the stuff your company sells? And what if everyone else's raise at most every other company in the country also comes from the newly increased price of the stuff their companies sell?

Gee, guess what? You got a 7% raise . . . and the price of everything you buy just went up 10%. You now have less money than when you started—a state otherwise known as inflation.*

▪ **And why is there never enough money?**
Your company always wants to make more money this year than it made last year. The most common way to do that is to sell more stuff to the people who already buy it and find other people to sell it to who have never bought it before.

Now, let's turn the tables. Let's talk about the company in the offices down the hall. They, too, want to make more money this year than they did last year. And the best way for them to do that is to sell more stuff to the people who already buy their stuff and to find new people to whom they can sell it.

Well, you've never bought their stuff before. *But, hey, look at this neat thing-a-ma-jig they've got!* you say to yourself one day. *I really need one of those.* And you buy it.

Meanwhile, when your friend Bert sees you with your new thing-a-ma-jig he says, "Oh, wow! You got the new and improved thing-a-ma-jig! That's way better than my thing. Mine's a couple of years old already. I've got to get the upgrade."

Doesn't it seem like there is always some new-and-improved something coming out that you've just got to have? Yet how are you supposed to have them when your puny monthly income is already stretched to the limit?

▪ (Repeat the following in your most annoying whine) **Why can't I have as much as my neighbor?**
You probably can. But what are you willing to give up to get it? Are you willing to go further into debt? Are you willing to work until 8? Or take a second McJob? Or stop eating in restaurants? Or clip coupons out of the Sunday paper? Or turn down the heat in your house?

---

* Actually, this example is about one type of inflation: demand-pull. One other type of inflation is called cost-push. But we'll talk about that later on.

How about doing all of these things? It's a pretty sure bet that if you started managing your money in a different way, you could be the proud owner of all the same stuff.

By the way, a French economist named Jean Baptiste Say (1767–1832) concluded that the more you take into the market, the more you get to take from the market. Although at first it is tempting to respond to Say's law with a resounding "Duh!" the reality is that the law has many layers of subtlety.

First and most obvious is that if you make five widgets and sell them in the marketplace you'll have more cash in your pocket than if you sell three widgets (actually, it's not really that simple, but we'll get to that when we talk later about supply and demand).

On the other hand, what you also need to consider is that the very act of producing more widgets creates more work for others (after all, you need labor and parts to put those widgets together), and this increase in economic activity reverberates throughout the entire economy.

The moral of the story: If you want to own as much stuff as your neighbor, get to work and produce more stuff to take to the marketplace.

IT AIN'T "SCHOOLHOUSE ROCK," BUT . . .

To explain economics in more accessible terms, we give you the economist's song cycle on scarcity:

"You Can't Always Get What You Want"
—THE ROLLING STONES

"[Money] Can't Buy Me Love"
—THE BEATLES

"What's Love Got to Do with It?"
—TINA TURNER

Some truths don't need further explanation.

■ **Will I ever get ahead by asking these questions?**

Many economists call economics the science of common sense because once you take the time to sit down and think about it, it's really pretty simple and clear. The problem is, most people never sit down and think about it, so many of the great mysteries of life, like "Hey! Where has all my money gone?" and "Where does my money come from?," et cetera and so forth, remain giant mysteries to the bitter end.

■ Does economics always look this dismal?

Yup.

Economists are usually looking at constraints, tradeoffs, and opportunity costs, all subjects that tend not to be the main subjects of motivational speeches. Just look at the first two truths: (1) money is earned and (2) there's no free lunch. Ugh! Instead of contemplating these truths, most people would rather dream of hitting that winning lottery number. In fact, economics has long been called the dismal science, a name which comes from the writings of Scottish essayist and historian Thomas Carlyle. Carlyle coined the phrase when writing about the perennial pessimist Thomas Malthus and his gloomy belief that our ever-expanding exponential population growth and limited food supply would someday result in worldwide famine.

> **. . . AND NOW, THE PUNDITS' VIEWS**
>
> What this country needs is a really good five-cent cigar.
> —U.S. VICE PRESIDENT THOMAS MARSHALL (1913–1921)
>
> There are plenty of good five-cent cigars in the country. The trouble is they cost a quarter. What this country really needs is a good five-cent nickel.
> —JOURNALIST FRANKLIN P. ADAMS

Although the basic laws of economics may go relatively unchanged over time, some mechanisms within the economy seem to change dramatically.

Or do they?

When radio became a popular entertainment medium in the 1920s, it must have struck listeners as odd that once they bought the radio itself, they never had to pay to enjoy the programming again. However, by the time television became popular 30 years later, people had grown accustomed to this concept of "free" broadcast entertainment.

But is it really free? Let's look at this

> **One view:**
>
> The times change and we change with them.
> —ROMAN EMPEROR LOTHAIR I (C.E. 795–855)
>
> **A dissent:**
>
> There's no such thing as a free lunch.
> —ECONOMIST MILTON FRIEDMAN

issue of "free" deals by looking at the latest mass-consumption product of our time: the free Internet browser.

It's confusing, isn't it? You surf over to the Netscape or the Microsoft site and they give you "free" browser software. Wow! Then you surf over to the WinZip site and get their free file compression software. Cool!

Then you click your way over to the Yahoo! site and play a few games of backgammon (or poker or blackjack) for free.

What's going on?

Has the digital age turned Lothair into a seer and Milton into a liar? Or could this just be a case of the same old same old dressed in the emperor's new clothes?

We're going to get into Milton Friedman's corner on this one.

From our perspective, "free" software and "free" games and all that other stuff you get off the Internet for free aren't really free at all. In fact, you pay for them just like we pay for watching traditional network TV.

You pay with your mind. With your time. Because every time you find something "free" on the 'net, there's almost sure to be some advertising attached.

Ah, you say. But what about things like Usenet groups and personal home pages that are filled with loads of information and advice, but no advertising? Isn't that info free?

Well, yes.

But there's a price you'll pay for taking any of that "free" information or advice.

For instance, if the "free" advice is also bad advice, who are you going to sue for malpractice? Or what if you get a computer virus while you're downloading a file full of "free" advice and lose all the data on your hard drive?

You'll notice that "free" advice on the web doesn't come with any guaran-

---

CASHING IN ON THE WEB

We don't mean to say that the Internet doesn't offer some wonderful opportunities for entrepreneurs. Yet the principles that are helping on-line companies grow are the same principles that have always worked for businesses. To learn more about these principles, see marketing guru Jay Conrad Levinson's books *Guerrilla Marketing: Secrets for Making Big Profits from Your Small Business*, *Guerrilla Marketing Attack: New Strategies, Tactics, and Weapons for Winning Big Profits for Your Small Business*, and *Guerrilla Marketing Online: The Entrepreneur's Guide to Earning Profits on the Internet* (coauthored with Charles Rubin).

tees. So if you have any problems, you have got nowhere to turn. And what it costs for you to set things right is one of the costs of that "free" advice.

Yes, it's possible to get useful information off the web. But even when it's good, there's still a price attached . . . and what that price will be will vary in every case. It might be the price of peace of mind, for instance. Once you take free advice, do you then fret and worry about the quality of the advice or the consequences of having taken the free advice should it turn out to be bad?

Ultimately, it comes down to the law of self-interest once again. If something goes wrong, if you find out the "good" advice you got was good but not good enough, if . . . if . . . if . . . Are you willing to bear the consequences?

Finally, we also have to say that even if you regard info on the web from Usenet groups and personal home pages as free, in spite of the costs we've outlined here, the fact that such information is free is nothing new.

They call the 'net the 'net because it's a network, and people have been networking to gather and exchange information since the beginning of time.

Before the advent of the Internet, you could have gotten the exact same information for free by calling friends, friends of friends, fan clubs, owner groups, retailers, wholesalers, distributors, service organizations, trade organizations, your representative in Congress, and so on—folks that you find today by surfing the web. The only difference is, the web makes that info a little easier to find. (Or does it? By the time you get past all the busy signals and actually get on-line, then search Yahoo!, Excite, InfoSeek, WebCrawler and Alta-Vista, looked at 20 or 30—or 200 or 300—sites and finally find what you're really looking for, how much time have you really saved?)

WHO PUT THE "CAPITAL" IN "CAPITALISM"?

You might be interested to know it was none other than Karl Marx, the father of communism and the author of the *Communist Manifesto* written with Friedrich Engels, and *Das Kapital,* who gave capitalism its name.

Just in case you haven't already figured this out, when we talk about economics, what we are mostly talking about—in this book, anyway—is the system of economics called capitalism.

But don't be frightened or intimidated by that word. In fact, we're betting you know a lot more about capitalism than you think you do—especially if we put you to the test against someone who was raised in a communist country.

Take Mikhail Gorbachev, for instance.

As Dimitry Zarechnak, a Russian interpreter for the U.S. Department of State, tells it:

> I was on *Marine One,* the president's helicopter, with President [George H. W.] Bush and President [Mikhail] Gorbachev. We were on our way back to the White House from Camp David. President[s] Bush and Gorbachev were seated on one side of the aisle facing each other across the table and I was seated on the other side of the aisle interpreting for them.
>
> At one point in the conversation they both ran out of things to talk about. They had been up at Camp David together, neither had anything more to say, and because they were facing each other it was a little bit awkward.
>
> I figured, "Well, maybe I can step in and ease the awkwardness."
>
> As it happened, we were flying over Silver Spring, Maryland, where I live. So I said to Gorbachev, "My house is just about down there." And he started asking me questions about how much it cost when I bought it, how much it was worth now, and things like that. I answered his questions and filled President Bush in about what was going on so he would know. President Bush suggested to Gorbachev, "Just ask one of your aides to get a newspaper and I'll show you all the houses for sale. I'll show you all the ads for real estate brokers." And Gorbachev said, "In our country this would be considered to be a crime, to be a real estate broker."

Dimitry and President Bush continued to explain the mechanics behind Western-style real estate and home ownership, something most of us easily take for granted, to President Gorbachev for the rest of the trip back to the White House.

So you still think you've got a lot to learn about capitalism?

If you are reading this and you grew up in the Western (largely capitalistic) world, you have a huge advantage over people who did not. Because it turns out that unlike breathing, capitalism is not innate.

Concepts that anyone with a high school education or higher in this country take for granted—supply and demand, the importance of good customer service, the mechanisms of a car or home loan, for instance —were, until recently, utterly foreign ideas to the vast majority of people in the former USSR and many other people all over the world.

And for most people in those countries who grew up under a state-run economy, making the change hasn't been easy.

It wasn't enough that their governments gave them permission to live and work in a free-enterprise system after years of having the economy micromanaged by the state. The population under that economic system had no idea what *free enterprise* meant.

"Fundamental principles that may seem obvious to Westerners aren't necessarily obvious to Russians," Patricia W. Hamilton, an editor for Dun & Bradstreet reports, recalled when writing of her first trip to Russia with an organization called the Alliance of American and Russian Women. "Take, for example, the idea that a successful enterprise must offer a product or service that meets a need . . . [or the concept of] credit and how it functions in business."

In other words, stuff we all take for granted was a complete mystery to many Russians as the curtain of communism fell at their feet.

"MY DAD'S ECONOMY CAN LICK YOUR DAD'S ECONOMY!"

Obviously our economy is different from the economy of the former Soviet Union . . . which calls to mind the following question: What is an economy and how many different kinds of economies are there?

In the driest terms possible, an economy is the combination of two things:

- the difference between what an entity earns and what that same entity spends, whether that entity is a 4-year-old child or a billion-dollar corporation;
- the goods and services this entity produces to earn what it does

and the goods and services the same entity consumes when it spends what it does.

Which leaves us with another question: What is an entity? Nations are entities. So are states, in the case of the United States. So are regions and cities and towns and counties. You are an entity, too.

Technically speaking, economies come in three different flavors:

- You know you live in a traditional economy if you feed and support yourself the same way your parents did—and it involves a simple technology like hunting or fishing or the gathering of plant matter.

- You know you live in a command economy if someone (usually a government official or agency) tells you where to live, where to work, what you can buy, and how much of it you can have.

- You know you live in a market economy if you can do almost any darn thing you want to earn a living (or do nothing and earn no living at all) and spend your money almost any darn way you choose.

EVERYTHING YOU ALWAYS WANTED TO KNOW ABOUT CAPITAL AND CAPITALISM

Capitalism $101

CAPITALISM: "Capitalism is a form of economic system in which most of the means of production—the factories, tools, equipment, coal mines, oil wells, railroads, and others—are owned by private individuals, not by the government. The owners are free to use their factories, mines, and all their other things in any way they wish. In general, people and businesses will seek to increase their profits. They will use their resources, energies, and tools in response to the market process. The workers and resource-owners who respond best—by making the things that society wants most—will enjoy the biggest incomes and profits. Those who do not do, or make, something to meet the wants of others, won't get anything."*

---

* Elbert V. Bowden, *Economics: The Science of Common Sense* (South-Western Publishing, 1974), 71.

Well, yeah, sure. But it does sound a bit like the Republican party platform for a presidential campaign. However, just as the Inuit have many different words to describe many types of snow, as capitalists we have many different names for many different flavors of capitalism. Here are a few of them:

- PURE CAPITALISM: Capitalism as described above. The market dictates how resources are allocated with little (or better yet, no) intervention from government.

- LAISSEZ-FAIRE CAPITALISM: Literally, *laissez faire* means "non-interference." From that you might surmise that laissez-faire capitalism and pure capitalism are one and the same—both forms of capitalism that exist without the helping hand of government.

- MIXED CAPITALISM: Reality, as applied to the definition of *capitalism* above. Take an economy that is mostly privately owned and mostly governed by the five laws of economics, then throw in some government regulation (for instance, fixed milk prices and tariffs on foreign imports) and you end up with mixed capitalism.

Anticapitalism $101

What types of economies are there on the philosophic other side of the economy tracks?

- SOCIALISM: Sort of like mixed capitalism, but with lots more governmental regulation and control. In a socialist economy, many means of production (factories, the raw materials, all modes of transportation, etc.) are owned by the government and many of the basic needs of the people are overseen by the government.

- COMMUNISM: An extreme version of mixed capitalism, with emphasis on the *mix* and less on the *capitalism*. The primary difference between mixed capitalism and communism is the degree to which one (mixed capitalism) tolerates some government intervention in economic affairs and the other (communism) requires almost absolute intervention. To that end, under a communist system private ownership of any of the means of production (except labor, of course) is outlawed. The government controls all aspects of supply, demand, production, distribution, pricing, and marketing, and income is distributed equally or on the basis of need.

THE ONE BOOK I WOULD READ . . .

Professionally, I would recommend a very technical book. It's not for everybody. It's only for professionals. John Hicks, *Value and Capital: [An Inquiry into Some Fundamental Principles of Economic Theory]*. It's a little dated — the problem with a technical field is that the great book is not necessarily the book you would recommend to read. The latest up-to-date exposition, which may be written by someone far inferior, may nevertheless be better to learn from.

Hicks'[s] *Value and Capital* is a remarkable book and I want people to read it. In a nutshell, it's the clarity of thinking—he saw some complicated issues that people had a lot of trouble even conceptualizing and he made them something everybody could understand. When I say everybody, I mean everybody in the field. It's not a book for laymen. Today, I would give it to a good undergraduate senior. When it was written, of course it was far beyond that. Books like that always have a tendency to become easier to understand with time.

—KENNETH J. ARROW, WINNER OF THE 1972 NOBEL PRIZE FOR ECONOMICS

ECON AS ART

William F. Sharpe, winner of the 1990 Nobel Prize for Economics, explains why he chose a career in economics over a career in the arts:

I guess what I really wanted to be was a photographer. I was a photographer for the high school annual and I was very hooked on such things. I used to hang around camera stores and things of that sort . . . (but) a guy who ran a camera store in town advised me you couldn't make money at that, which turned out to be true—they went bankrupt later on. . . . A photographer I hung around a bit explained to me you couldn't make much money being a photographer, so at some point in high school I decided maybe that wasn't for me.

OR IS IT ART AS ECON?

The aforementioned William Sharpe goes on to explain why a career in the arts does pay, even when it barely pays:

> I'm operating out of my field of expertise to some extent. . . . It [art] is not an area where you have the kinds of production gains you have making widgets or computers. By definition, I guess, it is a labor-intensive field. So that puts it, in a sense, at a disadvantage against competing products where you have production gains and technology improves things, and such. . . . The key thing is, it's so damn much fun, people are willing to do it for nothing or next to nothing. One of the reasons you don't earn much in that business, even if you do it professionally, is it's so much fun and there are plenty of talented people who will do it for low income.

What's Money Got to Do with It?

This might be a good time to talk about "opportunity costs." Simply put, it works like this: every time you exercise your right to do what is best for you—a.k.a. invoking the law of self-interest— then you are also, by necessity, choosing not to do something else. Nobelist William F. Sharpe ultimately chose to be an economist because, in the long run, he felt that would be the best choice for him. What was the opportunity cost associated with this choice? What did he give up? He didn't get to pursue his dream of being a photographer.

On the other hand, as Sharpe points out, those crazy artists seem to be ignoring the common-sense rules of society and working real hard at their art for free or darn near free instead of doing something worthwhile for a healthy paycheck. In the case of these artists, that opportunity cost is a respectable wage.

Other examples: One of your authors chose to study economics, so he studied more and wrote po-

DEEP POCKETS

When a socialist harangued Andrew Carnegie about redistribution of wealth, Carnegie asked his secretary for two numbers— the world's population and the value of all his assets. He divided the latter by the former then said to his secretary, "Give this gentleman 16 cents. That is his share of my net worth."

—JOURNALIST GEORGE WILL

etry less; Michael Jordan chose to play professional basketball and, as a result, he never found out if he could really learn to hit a major-league curveball; billions of tax dollars are spent on national defense, leaving less resources for other publicly funded programs. There may be value to the things we choose to do. However, regardless of what we choose to do, we always give up something else; hence, there's no such thing as a free lunch.

THE $5 HISTORY OF ECONOMICS

Are goods good? Early thinkers disagreed:

- In his *Republic,* Plato gave two thumbs down to the idea of private property.

- Aristotle, in his *Politics,* gave the notion of private property two thumbs up.

- Fast-forward about a thousand years: Saint Thomas Aquinas was all for private property and free trade as long it was all done in a moral and just way. You could say he was procapitalism but antigreed: He didn't mind if people engaged in trade as long as everyone got a fair shake in the deal.

> For a wonderful spiritual antidote for all the material-world analysis found in the economic field, see *Money and the Meaning of Life,* by philosopher (not economist) Jacob Needleman.

THE END OF DUTY FREE; OR, THE BIRTH OF BRITISH, FRENCH, AND GERMAN MERCANTILISM

Here's how it worked: From the 1500s to the late 1700s, the English, French, German, and other major European governments each ruled their national economies with an iron hand. The goal of each nation was to make sure that exports exceeded imports. The theory was that wealth was in limited supply, and that you could get ahead only at everyone else's expense. Therefore, if you were selling more to the outside world than you were buying, you'd be getting fatter and happier while the other countries were getting leaner and poorer.

Meanwhile, gold and silver were used to balance the books, so countries with gold and silver mines could also maintain their wealth by digging deeper into the ground. Countries without any gold or silver resources would have to take drastic steps to avoid slipping further and further behind.

Those steps included putting high tariffs on imported goods, establishing overseas colonies to establish new markets for exports, and exploiting territories for new or valuable raw materials. To ensure that there would always be a strong and willing workforce, governments also encouraged rapid population growth. Of course, that growing population provided an expanding market for domestic products as well.

ADAM SMITH'S WEALTH OF NATIONS

You think the Russians were confused after the former Soviet Union changed from a command economy to a market economy?

At least they had a lot of nice Americans hanging around, willing to take the time to explain things to them.

In Adam Smith's time (1723–1790), no one understood anything about anything. From the casual (or even academic) observer's point of view, the economy of England was a seething mass of chaos. People pushing and shoving their way into the streets to buy, people elbowing and jostling their way into the streets to sell. It was madness! No one was controlling what was for sale and no one was regulating what was being bought. What a mess.

That's where Adam Smith came in.

Some were concerned that such an economy—a market economy with no governmental control or order—could lead only to shortages, rioting and trouble. Smith, however, calmly explained in his book *An Inquiry into the Nature and Causes of the Wealth of Nations* that even though the government was not controlling the economy, order was actually being maintained. In spite of chaos in the marketplace, Smith explained, through some almost magical or mystical means, buyers found sellers who were selling what they wanted at an acceptable price . . . and sellers were finding buyers for what they had to sell at an acceptable price.

Of course, the words *magical* and *mystical* have no place in the study of so profound a science as economics. So Adam Smith explained that the economy and its seemingly naturally occurring sense of order was being guided by "an invisible hand."

Smith's point is easy to grasp in the entrepreneurial times in which we live.

Let's say you have an idea for a product. Let's call it the Home-Style Electrodigital Bubble Gum Machine (HSEDBGM). The perfect holiday gift. You are sure everyone in the world will want one. So you open a small factory in your garage and start making them.

Pretty soon, demand for the HSEDBGM is so great you have to open a new plant at the industrial park down the road. But demand continues to grow at a rate that far exceeds your production ability.

Uh, oh! Christmas is coming. You have to get 10 zillion more HSEDBGMs manufactured and delivered to stores. So you find a plant that can make them abroad.

Meanwhile, Black & Decker, General Electric, Starbucks, Radio Shack, Braun, Sony, Mitsubishi, and DreamWorks SKG (they want to give their HSEDBGMs away at a fast-food chain as part of an animated movie tie-in) take note of your incredible success and come out with their own versions of the personal HSEDBGM in time to meet holiday demand.

With supply so high and so many brands and models to choose from, the price of personal HSEDBGMs plummets. Pretty soon, even the poorest of the poor can afford to own a HSEDBGM, or at least a HSEDBGM Jr. or a HSEDBGM Express or a HSEDBGM Mini or a HSEDBGM Lite.

Without a single government bureaucrat pulling a single governmental string, the "invisible hand" made it possible for everyone who wanted a HSEDBGM to get one—and there is at least one model available at every conceivable price point.

The same can be said for lots of other stuff, such as sport utility vehicles, personal computers, cellular phones, DVD (digital video disc) and DVIX machines, and Thighmasters.

Bring the invisible hand into focus by visiting the original source: See the Modern Library edition of Adam Smith's great work, *An Inquiry into the Nature and Causes of the Wealth of Nations.*

ALEXANDER HAMILTON'S BANK OF NEW YORK AND OTHER ADVENTURES IN ECONOMICS

What a smart dude. First, in 1784, Hamilton laid the groundwork and then drew up the plans for the Bank of New York, which predated other commercial banks in the United States by more than 15 years.

A few years later, in 1789, George Washington made Hamilton the first secretary of the treasury. And along with the job, Hamilton inherited a big problem.

THIS DEBT IS YOUR DEBT; THIS DEBT IS MY DEBT . . .

You might be interested to know that the debts that Alexander Hamilton began to incur on behalf of the United States of America in 1789 were finally paid off by President Andrew Jackson in 1835— and to date, President Jackson has been the only president who has ever been able to pay off the national debt. It had never happened before 1835 and it hasn't happened since.

The country had just won its independence . . . but was deep in debt. To pay off its debts, the country had to produce lots of stuff and sell it. In addition, each of the 13 colonies (or states, at that point) had its own currency, which made things confusing and hindered trade.

Hamilton's cure was to open a national, central bank.

With the founding of the Bank of the United States in 1791, Hamilton was able to accomplish three things:

- He gave the people a network of linked banks at which they could deposit their money—and made it possible for citizens of all colonies to use the same currency as a universal medium of exchange.

- By dipping into those deposits,* he made it possible for new businesses to form and existing businesses to expand by making capital available to them in the form of loans.

- He created a secure and dependable source of credit for the new government that enabled the country to develop and grow. Without this line of credit, it would have been impossible for the colonies to build roads and bridges and all that other stuff you need to make a strong infrastructure.

---

* Does "dipping into those deposits" sound suspicious to you? If so, wait until you read more, later on, about the banking industry and the Federal Reserve.

THE ONE BOOK I WOULD READ . . .

One of the classics, and you can tell it's a classic because it's always invoked and rarely read, is the argument for the form of government that we have which is laid out in *The Federalist* papers. It's just not read and it's great stuff. *The Federalist* papers were written by Alexander Hamilton, James Madison, and John Jay in 1787 as a defense of the Constitution. They asked, "What is this Constitution that we have proposed for this country and how will it work?"

What they get into is our theory of government; representation, checks and balances, the [p]residency, and the courts. It is essentially the doctrine, teaching, and ideas behind our form of government, and it's actually pretty good reading. It is the intellectual framework for free government and it is very rarely read.

—WILLIAM J. BENNETT, FORMER U.S. SECRETARY OF EDUCATION, EX−DRUG CZAR, AND AUTHOR OF *THE BOOK OF VIRTUES: A TREASURY OF GREAT MORAL STORIES*

TAKE A RIDE ON READING: EXPANDING TOWARD THE INDUSTRIAL REVOLUTION

"The American people [are] . . . devoured by a thirst for riches . . ." said Frenchman Alexis de Tocqueville, author of *Democracy in America* (written between 1835 and 1840)—and that thirst was being fed by the expansion of the railroad.

For rich guys like Cornelius Vanderbilt, James Fisk, and Jay Gould, the railroads provided a springboard to expand into the realm of megawealth. These three men controlled the railroad (thanks to them and others like them, we now have strict antitrust laws in place), and they controlled virtually all the commerce of the nation as well. As the nation grew—in terms of boundaries, population, and commerce—the railroad was needed to move raw materials around and then to take finished goods to the nation's markets.

The railroads contributed to the rapid growth of the nation in another way. Every time the railroad moved farther away from the established East Coast, in this new place there would be a greater need for labor and steel and train cars and locomotives and tracks. This would lead to more need for food and clothing and housing and oil and liquor. Which led to more need for labor, which led to the need for more industry, other than the railroad, which was really just passing by as an industry, on its way to the next startup, along-the-side-of-the-tracks new town.

SONGS IN THE KEYNES OF LIFE

Adam Smith's take on economics sounded good for a long, long time. In fact, you can still hear many—often Republicans—advocating his laissez-faire "Hey, government, keep your hands off the economy" approach to economics.

Then in 1929, along came the Great Depression. And John Maynard Keynes.

Keynes questioned Adam Smith's concept of "the invisible hand."

In 1930s America, unemployment was stratospheric, production was almost nonexistent, and the two kept feeding off one another. It was a vicious spiral. The fewer jobs there were, the less people bought, and the less people bought, the fewer jobs there were. Things were looking mighty grim.

In 1936, Keynes wrote *The General Theory of Employment, Interest, and Money* and turned the whole world of economics on its head.

"How could it be," Keynes asked, "that millions of people could be willing to work, yet unable to find jobs? Aren't the unemployed really just sellers of labor looking for buyers of their work? And if there truly were an invisible hand, wouldn't it guide them to the place where their labor was needed?"

Clearly, Keynes had a point.

He also had a solution in mind: government intervention.

In particular, Keynes argued that if the market economy wasn't producing enough jobs, then the government should spend money to create jobs. What should the government spend money on? Well, according to Keynes, almost anything would work. In fact, he's purported to have advocated hiring people to dig holes and hiring other people to fill them up. Anything to get people working, earning a paycheck, and buying stuff. In fact, the application of Keynes's ideas in the Great Depression led to lots of beautiful and practical stuff other than just holes in the dirt—for instance, the National Parks system and the Golden Gate Bridge.

HOW TO START YOUR OWN DEPRESSION

The Great Depression came about because of wild speculation in the marketplace while certain key industries—like coal mining and shipbuilding—were stagnating. Meanwhile, the banking industry was under-regulated and their lending policies were far too liberal.

And, of course, as with any economy, things change.

Banks began to be saddled with bad debts, so they tightened the money supply. But it was too late. Soon, they were crashing and burning. When money got tight, it got harder for businesses to continue operating at high levels. As businesses cut back on production, they ordered less raw materials and their inventories grew. As inventories piled up, the need for production decreased. The services of fewer workers were required. The stock market plummeted.

Suddenly, anyone with anything in the market had dramatically less money to spend. And the existing problems with banks and inventory and unemployment quickly began to spiral out of control. By the time it was over, 34,600 banks had failed and 12 million to 15 million people were out of work. Some people jumped out of windows in despair.

Back in the early days of the Depression, while Herbert Hoover was president and when macroeconomics was in its infancy, everyone thought the solution was to cut taxes, reduce the federal budget, and balance it. Poor Hoover! He will always be remembered as "the Depression president." The poor guy was so clueless as to how to dig the nation out of the Depression he began grasping at straws. Desperate for help, for an answer, for a solution, he once offered singer Rudy Vallee a medal if he would "sing a song that would make people forget their troubles and the Depression."

> As President Richard Nixon once said: "Now, we are all Keynesians."

Today, most presidents would approach the situation differently. Instead of looking to Rudy Vallee for an answer, they would follow the advice of John Maynard Keynes and do things that would stimulate the economy—such as lower interest rates and spend government money like there was no tomorrow.

The goal is to get people working and get businesses spending. This should start the wheels of production rolling again, which should get even more people working. And they would have money to spend. This would create a need for more production, which would create a need for *more* production and, hence, would create more jobs. It goes on and on and on . . . hopefully.

When Franklin Delano Roosevelt (a.k.a. FDR) took over the presidency from Herbert Hoover, he was determined to attack the problem differently. Hoover was an engineer by training. He looked at things analytically. FDR was a man of action. In his first inauguration speech in 1932, he made this promise: "I pledge to you, I pledge myself, to a new deal for the American people." The New Deal was born: FDR hit the ground running.

FDR AT BAT

"I have no expectation of making a hit every time I come to bat," President Franklin Delano Roosevelt once took the time to explain. "What I seek is the highest possible batting average."

He sent so many spending bills to Congress in his first 100 days in office that it was impossible to keep track of them. On the floor of Congress a ringing cry of "Vote! Vote!" could be heard through the halls as the nation's leaders approved project after project and fought to put the country back to work again. One Roosevelt aide spent $5 million dollars in his first two hours on the job. In just two months, the same aide created 4 million jobs.

"How Many Shopping Days till Christmas?"

Keynes, it turns out, was right—or at least President Roosevelt thought so. And one of the most amusing Keynesian steps FDR took to stimulate economic growth and spending was to change the date of Thanksgiving in 1939.

FDR reasoned that if people celebrated the holiday on the third Thursday of November instead of the traditional fourth Thursday, they would start their Christmas shopping that much earlier in the month and, he reasoned, that extra week of shopping certainly couldn't hurt.

THE ONE BOOK I WOULD READ . . .

There's the question, first of all, of what books have had an influence on me. Second, there's a question of whether I would recommend that people read them, and third, would I recommend that they read them now.

[John Maynard] Keynes'[s] book had a great influence on me, but I think it's a hell of a way to try to understand Keynesian economics. It's *The General Theory of* whatever it is . . . *General Theory of Employment, Income, and* something.

—HERBERT A. SIMON, WINNER OF THE 1978 NOBEL PRIZE FOR ECONOMICS

In my field, I suppose John Maynard Keynes'[s] 1936 classic *General Theory of Employment, Interest, and Money* would be the single most important book. I

guess the book in economics that's had the biggest impact on my life is my own elementary textbook. After I had a reputation at the frontier of the black esoteric arts of economics, I became author of a bestseller, so I can't go anywhere in the world where I don't run into somebody who says, "Oh, I used your book in Timbuktu, or Malaysia, or Tennessee." And the name of that book is *Economics*. I wrote it in 1948 and the fourteenth edition has just come out."
—PAUL ANTHONY SAMUELSON, WINNER OF THE 1970 NOBEL PRIZE FOR ECONOMICS

RICARDO, MALTHUS, MILL, AND MARX

First, *David Ricardo* (1772–1823) made a killing in the English stock market in his twenties; then he decided to become an economist. The way Ricardo saw it, the only way to judge the value of a product was to measure the amount of labor that was required to make it. This was good news for business but bad news for labor, for the other part of his theory was that no matter how strong the economy got, the plight of the laborer would never significantly improve.

In a prosperous economy, Ricardo believed, members of the working class might begin to get ahead and they would naturally have more children. By virtue of having more children, there would be an excess of labor when those offspring entered the workforce. This, of course, would drive wages back down.

The name *Thomas Robert Malthus* (1766–1834) has become synonymous with bad news, and here's why: He believed that given the rapid geometric ratio by which the human population grows and the slower arithmetic ratio that governs food production, humans will never be able to overcome poverty and hunger and despair. Not surprisingly, Malthus's theory about population had a tremendous influence on Charles Darwin and his theory of natural selection.

Along came *John Stuart Mill* (1806–1873). His father, James Mill, was the cofounder of the utilitarian movement, which was based on the belief that the goal of any public action should be the greatest happiness for the greatest number of people. When his father died, John Stuart took over as the leader of the movement. On the economic front, he supported the development of labor organizations to establish and protect workers' rights, emancipation for women, a system of cooperative agriculture, and other progressive ideas.

Karl Marx (1818–1883) considered it his job to give capitalism a bad name. As he saw it, all of history has been a class struggle between those who control resources and those who provide labor for those in control. Instead of a system of domination and exploitation, Marx believed that the means to produce all goods should be publicly owned.

A BRIEF HISTORY OF THE CORPORATION

Understanding the evolution of the corporation requires an understanding of the corporate entity itself.

In modern times, there are three basic forms of business ownership:

- THE SOLE PROPRIETORSHIP: The business is owned by one person, who provides the money to start the business (or borrows it as the sole creditor). When there is profit, it is the sole proprietor's money to take. When there is a loss, it comes out of the sole proprietor's pocket.

- THE PARTNERSHIP: A small number of people come together, pool their resources and skills, and operate a business. Partners may own equal shares of the business or the percentage of ownership may vary depending on how much capital or labor each partner invests. In any case, both the profits and losses of the business are shared between the partners. (We're fudging a bit here. There are actually many forms of partnerships. In the scenario above, all partners are general partners. There are other types of partnerships, such as the limited partnership, in which limited partners make an initial investment and share in the profits but can't be required to cough up more cash should the business go in the hole.)

- THE CORPORATION: Some number of people, ranging from one to a gazillion, each own some piece of the business. Ownership in the company comes in the form of a share of stock. (We'll talk about stocks and the stock market later on, on page 113.) Owning stock in a corporation is a bit like being part of a limited partnership—you made your initial investment and, should the corporation distribute profits, you will get a piece

HIDE THE MONEY—THE LAWYERS ARE COMING!

Here's another way corporations differ from partnerships and sole proprietorships: Sole proprietors and general partners are legally liable for the actions of their businesses. If the business borrows money and can't pay it back, the lender can sue the proprietor or partners for it. If the business is sued for some other reason—let's say someone loses a finger while using one of your widgets and files suit—it is the same as if the proprietor or partners were being sued personally. They can lose personal assets (like a house, car, boat, shares of stocks), as well as the assets of the business, in a lawsuit.

The corporation, on the other hand, gets a much sweeter deal. If it borrows money and can't pay it back or is sued because someone loses a finger, only the corporation itself can be held liable. The people who own the corporation—the stockholders—are completely sheltered from liability.

of the action. However, should the corporation lose money, it can't come to you and make you pony up.

If you stop and think about it, you'll see that it is much easier for a corporation to raise money and grow than it is for the two other forms of businesses to do so. All the corporation has to do is to sell more stock or bonds. And if the corporation is a solid one, people will be eager to own a part of it, since they will reap any profits but avoid all liability.

When you consider the history of the corporation, these are two important points.

The history of the corporation begins in the late 1700s, during the period of British, French, and German mercantilism. As you'll recall, the ruling powers of England, France, and Germany heavily regulated their economies to ensure that exports would be greater than imports. A positive balance of trade, they believed, was the key to building wealth.

One way jolly old England controlled its economy was to decide who could and who couldn't start a corporation. In this way, the government directed growth by chartering trading companies like the Hudson's Bay Company and Massachusetts Bay Company and sending them to the New World to establish new colonies and lay claim to the region's raw materials.

From a capitalistic and entrepreneurial point of view, this was a problem. Yet even back in the good old days, whenever there was a problem there was sure to be a group of hungry and capitalistic lawyers hanging around. In a classic case of loophole-o-rama, British barristers sneakily invented a new and improved form of corporation that didn't require anyone to get permission from anyone else.

Over in the recently formed United States, they were doing things pretty much the same way things got done in England. If you wanted to start a corporation, you had to get permission from the state. Unlike England, however, the United States was supposed to be about democracy and freedom and one's right to the pursuit of truth, justice, and the American way. In 1811, therefore, the State of New York passed a law that made it possible for anyone who wanted to start a corporation to do so anytime as long as he or she satisfied some basic legal requirements. Soon, all the other states followed suit.

"MAKE MINE MONOPSONY!" YOUR FAVORITE -OPOLIES AND -OPSONIES DEFINED

MONOPOLY

A monopoly is a market in which there is only one seller. Because there is no competitor, the monopolist has a lot of influence over the price of the product being made. In other words, the monopolist can drive prices up.

NATURAL MONOPOLY

Sometimes, it just doesn't make sense for there to be more than one supplier of a particular good or service. A perfect example is your local water company. The only way a water company can supply water is to build a pipeline from its reservoir to every house and business within its service area. That takes a lot of time, money, and land. Would you really want some other company to start tearing up the roads in your town to lay down a duplicate pipeline system, all in the name of competition? A company, then, has a natural monopoly on its market when it just doesn't make sense for there to be more than one supplier of a particular good or service.

MONOPSONY

A monopsony is the exact opposite of a monopoly—regardless of how many suppliers there are, there is only one buyer. Take, for example, defense contractors who build highly sophisticated missile systems that are based on classified information and research. If these defense contractors sold their product to anyone other than the Pentagon, they could get in an awful lot of trouble. Of course, monopsonists (such as the Pentagon) have a lot of influence over price. In other words, they can drive the price of a product down. (Which makes those $600 toilet seats all the more puzzling, doesn't it?)

OLIGOPOLY

An oligopoly is a situation in which an industry is dominated by a small number of suppliers. Take the market for petroleum, for instance. Most of the world's petroleum comes from a handful of countries. The interesting thing about an oligopoly is that their product offerings are usually offered at or about the same price. When one cuts the price, the others will follow.

If the few suppliers hold the price high, it will tend to stay that way. On the other hand, it is conversely true that the only way an oligopoly can raise its price is if it knows in advance that the competition will follow. (Haven't you ever noticed that airlines all seem to change their prices on or about the same day . . . and their prices always seem to be about the same?)

COLLUSIVE OLIGOPOLY

A collusive oligopoly is when oligopolists (the few sellers in the market) get together and act like a monopolist. A classic example is the Organization of Petroleum Exporting Countries (OPEC).

HENRY FORD AND BILL GATES HAVE A COUPLE OF BETTER IDEAS

Much as the railroad made it possible for American business to grow west, Henry Ford and his Model T made it possible for common people to go east, west, or anywhere else they wanted. The Model T was revolutionary: It was remarkably cheap—by design—so almost anyone who wanted one could afford one.

With a covert push to sink competing forms of transportation (see "Who Framed Roger Rabbit" on page 49), the automobile companies succeeded in expanding the markets for their product. As public acceptance of the automobile rose and the price fell, the age of the automobile brought other new economic trends with it. Suddenly, people needed a place to buy gas and places to eat and sleep while on road trips. They needed tires and motor oil and mechanics and body shops.

The Model T made it possible for people to drive to work; therefore—with massive investment in highway construction—housing could extend further away from industrial and city centers. Hence, the suburbs were born, along with their cousin urban sprawl. The automobile also brought credit (remember Alexander Hamilton?) to the consumer. To make it possible for almost anyone to buy a car, carmakers invented the car loan.

Fast-forward a few decades and we find the computer changing lives as dramatically as the car once changed lives. Each successive generation of computers is better/faster/cheaper. (In fact, we saw a recent news magazine that hailed the dawn of the "disposable" computer in the $400 range—machines that are so cheap that you wouldn't hesitate to buy a new one on a whim and then throw it away when a new/better/faster one comes along and catches your eye). Just as the spread of the auto created a need for goods and services for people who were traveling away from home, today the Internet gives us the ability to work and to shop for goods and services without ever leaving our homes.

Meanwhile, many people are concerned about the environmental impact of our excessive reliance on the internal combustion engine and they worry that urban sprawl may never end. They wonder if the Internet might offer an environmentally sustainable solution to such problems as the explosive growth of suburbia and our perpetually clogged freeway systems.

WHO FRAMED ROGER RABBIT

If you want to learn about the dark side of economics, go rent the movie *Who Framed Roger Rabbit* again—buried deep within the plot of this movie is a subplot of huge economic proportions. Think back to the movie; do you remember who framed Roger Rabbit? And why?

His name was Doom—Judge Doom. He's also the one who killed

Eddie Valiant's brother Teddy, Maroon Cartoon Studios owner R. K. Maroon, and Marvin Acme, the guy who owned Toontown and made all those crazy Acme gadgets you always see in cartoons. Judge Doom framed Roger Rabbit and killed Maroon and Acme for one reason . . . but we'll let him tell you in his own words:

> JUDGE DOOM: Several months ago I had the good providence to stumble upon a plan of the city councils. A construction plan of epic proportions. They're calling it . . . a freeway.
> EDDIE VALIANT: A freeway? What the hell's a freeway?
> DOOM: Eight lanes of shimmering cement running from here to Pasadena. Smooth, straight, fast. Traffic jams will be a thing of the past.
> EDDIE VALIANT: So that's why you killed Acme and Maroon? For this freeway? You're kidding.
> JUDGE DOOM: Of course not. You lack vision. I see a place where people get off and on the freeway. On and off. Off and on. All day, all night. Soon where Toontown once stood will be a string of gas stations. Inexpensive motels. Restaurants that serve rapidly prepared food. Tire salons. Automobile dealerships. And wonderful, wonderful billboards reaching as far as the eye can see. . . . It'll be beautiful.
> VALIANT: Come on. Nobody's gonna drive this lousy freeway when they can take the Red Car [local trolley line] for a nickel.
> DOOM: Oh, they'll drive. They'll have to. You see, I bought the Red Car so I could dismantle it.

Judge Doom may be a fictional character (and a Toon at that!), but the phenomenon he's describing above really did happen.

The mass appeal of cars rests on a simple fact: Cars offer an affordable means of transportation for taking individuals wherever they want, whenever they want. A product with that kind of functionality was likely to be pretty popular no matter what happened. But just to be sure, proponents of the automobile and related industries worked deliberately to undermine competing forms of transportation, as Judge Doom did with Toontown's Red Car line.

For example, in the 1930s General Motors (GM), Firestone Tire & Rubber Company, and Standard Oil of California got together and started a company called National City Lines (NCL). Their mission was to buy regional rail companies across the country and shut them down. Over a span of 20 years, NCL purchased and gutted more than 100 of these regional transit systems; public rail service was history for millions of people in 45 different cities.

In Los Angeles, GM, Goodyear Tire & Rubber Company, and Phillips Petroleum bought a Southern California rail line and dismantled it. Interestingly—in an "art imitates life" sort of way—the L.A. transit system was called the Red Line.

In exchange for killing the competition, these three companies were found guilty of committing "conspiracy in restraint of trade" in 1947. Punishment was levied in the form of a $1 fine.

In about the same period, legislation was passed in the San Francisco Bay area to outlaw the existing ferry transit which efficiently transported passengers across the bay. Why the legislation? Because investors in the automobile-carrying bridges needed to ensure that enough people would get in their cars and pay the tolls to cross their bridges.

Now here's a question you might want to think about before the sequel of *Roger Rabbit* is released: We've invested trillions of dollars worth of resources in the twentieth century into a transportation infrastructure to enable individual consumers and laborers to conveniently travel to and from work and shopping venues on a daily basis. If people will be required to travel less and less in the coming century because of telecommuting and on-line commerce, what are the infrastructure projects that might attract public resources the way transportation has in the twentieth century?

GLOBAL MALLONOMICS

It was President Theodore "Teddy" Roosevelt who decreed that the business of America is business. That has never been more true than today.

In fact, if you look around, you begin to see that the business of America is actually the business of global business as our Gaps and Starbucks and Levis and Microsofts continue the process of expanding their operations into nearly every corner of the world.

And you think you're getting tired of seeing the same old brands and stores and logos everywhere you go? Then you really ought to take pity on poor Calvin Klein's daughter Marci, who reported to a member of the press: "Every time I'm about to go to bed with a guy, I have to look at my father's name all over his underwear."

Of course, we all know the price of admission to this mall-onomic game of high stakes: if you want to be a part of it and make your own pile of riches, you'd better have an MBA—or least sound like you do.

HOW TO TALK LIKE AN MBA

If you wear the right shoes and the right suit and pepper your conversation with a few key phrases, no one will ever know you never got any farther than PS 129:

"THE LAW OF DIMINISHING RETURNS"

Definition: The additional output from an additional variable input will eventually decline, if some of the inputs are fixed in quantity.

Say what? Okay, let's try it this way: One Saturday, life gave your young daughter lemons, so she decided to open a lemonade stand. The stand was a hit and had a line around the block. In fact, she had to send some customers away empty-handed. Others got impatient and left before they got to the front of the line. That night, your daughter counted her take—$10—and came to the conclusion that if she had a little help mixing and serving, she could probably sell a lot more lemonade—so she recruited her little sister to help the next day.

Sure enough, the lemonade was again a huge success. Thanks to the extra help from sis, the family biz sold three times more lemonade and your two daughters each earned $15 for the day.

All week long, your eldest daughter ponders how to improve lemonade sales even more. "Aha!" she says one evening and runs down the street to recruit the help of Karl, the neighbor boy. With his help, she reasoned, she should be able to sell even more lemonade and make even more money!

Saturday comes and the three kids have a great time mixing and selling lemonade. But at the end of the day, a problem comes up: Sales have gone up, but the amount of the rise has declined. Whereas your eldest earned $10 the first day and the two girls each earned $15 the second day—for a total of $30 between them—on the third day the three kids earned only $40—so each of them made only $13.33.

What happened? The neighbor boy did help sell more lemonade ($40 is more than $30) but the extra sales were less than the extra sales that came from when the other worker (little sis) was added. In other words, the third worker's marginal productivity was less than the second worker's marginal productivity. In fact, if you think about it, if your daughter keeps adding more and more helpers to the single lemonade stand (that is, the input of fixed quantity), then the earnings per helper will continue to get smaller and smaller; each successive helper has less space in which to mix and serve.

Suddenly, the law of diminishing returns has become quite obvious to you . . . which is a good thing, since you now have to explain it to your kids.

"ECONOMIES OF SCALE"

As you've seen, adding more helpers to a single lemonade stand leads, eventually, to diminishing returns.

But, Mr. or Ms. MBA, who says you need to stick with a single outlet?

If you play the game right, your costs should go down as you grow. That's why McDonald's, Wal-Mart, and Home Depot are successful. Of course, part of the benefits from increasing scale is that you can buy everything you need in bulk and therefore lower your costs. But this source of savings isn't what economists refer to when they claim that economic benefits can come from increasing the scale of a business (that is, economies of scale).

Economies of scale come from opportunities for specialization. So what does that mean? Well, think about your daughter's lemonade stand. With one outlet, your daughter is CEO, human resources director, inventory control manager, product quality manager, advertising manager, treasurer, cashier, counter person, customer service representative, and lemon squeezer, filling many positions all at once. With a larger scale of operations—say a stand on every third corner in town—some of these roles are filled by individuals specializing in whatever function they happen to be filling, from CEO to lemon squeezer.

In this particular case, your daughter plays CEO; her sister plays human resources director, recruiting and hiring all the kids in the neighborhood; Karl becomes advertising manager and specializes in attracting customers through innovative campaigns involving loud-speakers, T-shirts on neighborhood dogs, and flyers at the local school. And other kids in the 'hood squeeze lemons.

In some industries, increased specialization arising from in-creased scale of business can lead to lower average production costs. Lemonade might be one of these industries. However, we kind of suspect that economies of scale are not very applicable to lemonade stands, since we don't see many large-scale operations. In other words, your daughter might engage in all that expansion and spe-cialization and, in the end, find out that average costs haven't re-ally been lowered very much. On the other hand, the production of fast–food hamburgers seems to result in very large economies of scales as evidenced by the experience of McDonald's, Wendy's, and Carl's Jr.

> The fashion of the world is to avoid cost . . .
> —WILLIAM SHAKESPEARE

In fact, the whole issue depends on the technology being used: Some tech-nologies have large economies of scale (anything with a production line, from cars to burgers), whereas others (any-thing that requires labor that can't be mechanized, from dentistry to handmade macrame plant holders) don't.

Being a rabid MBA-to-be, you know your main job in life is to stamp out costs while promoting income and earnings. But costs are sort of like cockroaches. Even though we'll never eliminate them completely, there's a certain satisfaction to be found in eliminating one whenever the opportunity arises. And here's another thing costs and cockroaches have in common: Whenever you see one, you can bet there are hundreds more hiding nearby.

"FIXED COST"

A fixed cost is a cost of doing business that is constant, regard-less of other levels of production or productivity. The perfect ex-ample of a fixed cost is rent. If the rent for a real estate office is $1,000 per month, the real estate company will pay $1,000 per month whether it sells one house in a month or 100. Fixed cost is also known as overhead. Now, compare fixed cost with . . .

. . . "VARIABLE COST"

Variable cost is the total of all costs that increase as your level of work increases. Notice we didn't say variable costs increase as productivity increases. Here's why: Let's go back to our real estate company. Let's say it advertises 10 houses in the paper this month but sells only one. Meanwhile, last month, it advertised only three houses in the paper but sold all three. The company was obviously more productive last month, although its variable costs will be much higher this month because it is doing significantly more advertising. Examples of other variable costs: the gasoline a realtor burns while driving clients to various houses, the cost of long-distance phone calls to out-of-town clients, the cost of printing and photocopying of fliers for the houses that are for sale.

"VARIABLE COST PER UNIT" AND "TOTAL VARIABLE COST"

Let's say that while you're working on your MBA, you notice just how many others around the country are working on their MBAs. Applying everything you have learned thus far in business school, you decide to capitalize on all these matriculating master's degree candidates and open a tassel factory.

You throw open the doors of your factory and a few months later notice something odd: In the slow month of January, variable costs per unit were higher than in February, but total variable costs were lower. You puzzle over this for a while but finally come to understand—in January you made 5,000 tassels and in February you made 20,000 tassels. When you analyze your variable costs, you see that you really don't benefit from an economy of scale until you reach a production run of about 10,000 tassels. Therefore, your variable costs per unit for 5,000 tassels is $0.20, double the variable cost per unit of a production run of 20,000. On the other hand, even though your variable costs per unit were higher in January, you didn't make nearly as many tassels that month, so the total variable cost was significantly less than it was in February.

"TOTAL COST" AND "TOTAL COST PER UNIT"

Okay, Mr./Ms. MBA and tassel-factory owner, chew on this for a while: If you add your fixed costs to your variable costs, you get total costs. If you divide your total cost by the number of tassels produced, you get total cost per unit.

For instance, let's say that in January fixed costs were $500, variable costs were $500, and we produced 5,000 tassels. Total cost for the month is $1,000 and total cost per unit is $0.20:

$$\frac{\text{Fixed Cost} + \text{Variable Cost}}{\text{Units Produced}} = \frac{\$500 + \$500}{5,000} = \$0.20$$

In February, on the other hand, fixed costs were $500, variable costs were $1,500, and we produced 20,000 tassels. Total cost per unit then is 10 cents:

$$\frac{\text{Fixed Cost} + \text{Variable Cost}}{\text{Units Produced}} = \frac{\$500 + \$1,500}{20,000} = \$0.10$$

Once again, our total cost is higher in February but our cost per unit is lower. Therefore, when we sell our tassels, we will earn a greater profit on the units produced in February than we will on the units produced in January.

"MARGINAL REVENUE"

Marginal revenue is the additional revenue you receive if you make and sell an additional unit of output.

That's easy, right? Any MBA knows that the additional revenue from an additional unit is "whatever the heck I sell it for" or, in other words, "the price of the product."

Well, pretty smart, Mr. or Ms. MBA. But of course you're only half right because you're only an MBA and not an economist. Let us explain.

Suppose you're a small producer of tassels in a market that produces millions and millions of tassels. And in this market, a tassel is a tassel is a tassel is a tassel. In other words, they're all exactly the same and each of them sells for $0.40. Well, in the world of small tassel production, your answer is correct: Price equals marginal revenue, which equals $0.40. You make another tassel and sell it and what do you get? That's right: $0.40.

But what about a market in which you're not such a small producer? Suppose you're a big fat monopolist or oligopolist. Now, the law of demand affects your marginal revenue.

"Huh?" you reply.

Surely you remember the law of demand: "The more of it there is to go around, the less people are willing to pay for it." This is the law you use to your advantage if you are a monopolist: you produce less of something and its price goes up because no one else is making it. But, of course, the law works in reverse, too. If you're a monopolist and you make more tassels, then—surprise!—there're more of them to go around and people expect to pay less. So, price falls. Take oil, for example: When one of the big producers sucks more of it out of the ground, the price of crude drops.

"MARGINAL COST"

By now, you're getting the idea on this "marginal" thing, right? Marginal cost is the additional cost to make one more unit of output. So, does it cost you more, less, or the same amount to make another tassel? That's right! "It depends."

Now you're starting to sound like an economist!

You remember when your daughter added her sister to the lemonade assembly line? They got more productive at the margin. And this increased marginal productivity resulted in lower costs, at the margin. If you wanted to look at the audited financial statements from their operation, you could calculate it for yourself: Their marginal cost declined when your second daughter joined the business.

But what happened next? They added another worker. Why? To produce more output. Did they produce more output? Yes. How much did the additional output cost to make (that is, what was the marginal cost)? Well, in this case, the marginal costs went up, not down. (Trust us, we could e-mail you the audited financials, but it's not a pretty sight.)

Why'd they go up? You have it: the law of diminishing returns. There is a limit to how much lemonade your daughter can produce in her lemonade stand given the size of the stand and the state of technology that currently governs production, and other factors like these. Clearly, once that production limit is reached, there will be diminishing returns on any additional labor (like Karl), and marginal cost will rise.

THE COSTCO PRINCIPLE

You will recall that way back in your early days of economic education (that is, at the beginning of this book), we talked about the rules of supply and demand, which say that the more of something there is, the less people will have to pay for it. We have applied this rule to many things in the course of this book, from sneakers to your own labor, and now it is time to apply it to tassels, of all things.

Although everything we have said about your tassel-manufacturing operation above is true, we sort of made the assumption that you could sell an unlimited number of tassels at a fixed price of $0.40 apiece. Of course, we know this is an unrealistic expectation—after all, when you go to a store and buy a large quantity of one item, don't you expect to pay less for it than if you were just buying one?

For instance, if you buy a case of soda or wine, you expect to pay less per bottle than if you were to just buy one bottle. In fact, this concept spawned an entire industry in the 1990s, with the advent of Price Club/Costco stores and Office Depot/OfficeMax/Staples stores, where the consumer is rewarded with lower prices in exchange for buying toilet paper and paper towels and boxes of Cheerios in ridiculously large quantities.

Well, the same concept applies to the tassel business. Just as at Costco, clients will expect to be rewarded for placing large orders. Therefore, when a client has a short-term need for 20,000 tassels (which will cost him $0.40 apiece, or $8,000), the client may be tempted to order 30,000 tassels at a cost of $.35 apiece or $10,500 because he or she knows the additional tassels can be used eventually, yet he or she gets to save a lot of money on them right now.

But enough about your client. Let's talk about you. You need to be able to figure out just how much of a price break you can give at different purchase levels and at what point you can go no lower.

To make sense of this, let's go back to Costco and buy a case of wine. If a bottle of your favorite wine costs $10 but you can get a case of 24 bottles for $192, then you know you have just paid 20% less, or $8 per bottle. Now, what if you buy two cases? Would you expect to pay yet another 20% less, or $6.40 per bottle? Well, it's a nice idea, but don't expect the manager of the department to go for it. After all, there's a limit to how low he or she can go with the price . . . otherwise, the manager will be selling the wine for less than he or she paid for it!

Just as the manager of the wine department at Costco does, you need to know how low you can go and still make a profit—and the only way you can determine that is if you know how much it costs you to make your product.

SHAKESPEAREAN ECONOMICS: TO BE OR NOT TO BE?

Or, less poetically: When should a business call it quits?

Well, MBA candidate, if you think the answer is "when a business is losing money," you're wrong.

In fact, it is sometimes cheaper for a business to continue to operate at a loss than it is for the same business to shut its doors.

"But how can that be?" you may feel compelled to scream, just like Shakespeare's Hamlet, who had to agonize over the question "To be or not to be?"

First of all, if a business is doing well—making above-normal or normal profits—this question is hardly given much thought; after all, you don't need an MBA to know that as long as total revenue equals or exceeds total costs, the right thing to do is to keep pushing forward.

But the question gets substantially trickier when the business is losing money, because in these circumstances, it is sometimes best to keep going and sometimes best to shut down. And you can make the right decision only if you apply what you just learned about fixed and variable costs.

Suppose that each month your tassel factory is producing 20,000 tassels for $0.10 apiece. Fixed cost (say, rent) is $500, variable cost (say, labor) is $1,500, and total cost is $2,000:

$$\$500 \text{ [fixed]} + \$1,500 \text{ [variable]} = \$2,000 \text{ [total cost]}$$

If a tassel sells for only $0.09 on the market, you lose money each month. How much? Well, selling all 20,000 tassels brings in $1,800 in revenue:

$$\$.09 \times 20,000 = \$1,800$$

Therefore, each month you're losing $200:

$$\$1,800 - \$2,000 = -\$200$$

Negative profits are not what you like to see. Now, if you see red and don't take time to ponder the situation, you might conclude: Cease to be, shut down, close up shop.

The problem is, you still have your fixed costs to pay. How much is that? $500. Which would you rather lose each month: $200 or $500? We hope you concluded that losing less is better than losing more. And since this lower loss comes from staying in business, you keep making tassels. (At least until your lease expires and you can stop paying rent.)

Of course, if the price of tassels is only $0.075 apiece, then 20,000 tassels earns only $1,500:

$$\$0.075 \times 20,000 = \$1,500 \text{ a month}$$

You would lose $500 whether you stayed in business or not. That's why economists call this point—where total revenue exactly equals total variable costs—the shut-down point.

Here's the bottom line: If you want to be smart like Hamlet and make the right decision, just remember that as long as your revenue can cover all your variable costs and contribute something toward your fixed costs, you are better off operating the business than closing it.

HEAVY METAL: THE HISTORY OF HUMANKIND'S EFFORTS TO MAKE MONEY

Quick: What's money?

Money is not the gold buried in your yard. It's not the stock certificates locked up in your vault. And it's not the green-and-white paper in your wallet or the coins jingling around in your purse or pocket.

Yup, all that stuff serves as money. In some cases, we call it money. But money it ain't.

What money really is is a thing that you can use to get other things.

Your thing might be labor. You paint houses well and you exchange your services for other stuff: food, clothing, shelter. Your thing might be stuff. You braid great baskets. And you exchange your baskets for such stuff as food, clothing, shelter, and getting your house painted.

The history of money is interesting because early people had a lot better handle on money than we do today. After all, when was the last time you sat at your desk and, as you typed a memo (or whatever), thought to yourself, *Hey, if it takes me thirty minutes to type a memo and I make twenty dollars an hour, then I am being paid ten dollars to type the memo. And when I go to the store to buy socks, they cost ten dollars for a set of three; therefore, three pairs of socks cost one memo?*

This is not how most of us regard money. Nor do we think to ourselves, *Hey, my car payment is two hundred dollars, so for that I have to type ten memos every month.*

We don't think of it this way because we do stuff for money, put the money in the bank, then draw it out later to buy other stuff. There's only a distant connection between the work we do for the money and the stuff we use the money to buy.

In an earlier age, people raised chickens, gathered their eggs, took them into town or the village, and traded those eggs for wheat. The correlation was clear: I give the wheat seller a dozen eggs, and I get a bushel of wheat.

This raises an interesting point. When people traded eggs for wheat, the value was clear. When both parties agreed to the trade— let's say 12 eggs for one bushel of wheat—they were both agreeing that a dozen eggs were equal to a bushel of wheat.

In modern economies, currency is usually used to represent the fruits of our labors, so we don't have to use the fruits themselves. As a result, however, we don't stop to consider that when we accept a job at wage X we are entering into the same sort of agreement. We are saying that our eight hours a day is worth X number of eggs or bushels of wheat.

At the same time, when we shop, we rarely mentally connect our purchases with our efforts at work. (And if we did, we'd probably buy fewer new cars and fewer expensive pairs of tennis shoes.) But even in our modern economy, there still exists lots of direct trading of goods (or what economists call barter). For instance, the Anheuser-Busch company, which pays its employees with currency just like all other companies, also pays them with beer. In fact, every employee of Anheuser-Busch is entitled to four six-packs a month. And if you work for a clothing store and are entitled to a discount on any clothes you buy, then the store you work for is using clothes as money.

So far, however, we've really skirted the issue of money itself. What is it? Well, actually, money is used in a few ways.

■ Most important, it's a medium of exchange. And a darn good one, at that. After all, if you sit and type memos all day, how much hamburger do you think the butcher would give you for a sheaf of them? And what if your job was to assemble automobile transmissions? It would be mighty difficult to haul one down to the butcher shop every time you wanted to buy a steak.

■ Money also serves as an easy way to save over time. Think about it: What if we had no durable form of money and you were an egg farmer? Trying to save for a rainy day could turn into a pretty smelly business. It's much easier to sell your surplus eggs for money and stuff the money under your mattress than it is to save those extra eggs under your bed.

At the Pacific Union Club in San Francisco the kitchen staff scours all the coins brought into the building by members tainted with the commerce of the streets. Only after the coins have been thoroughly polished do the waiters presume to offer them as change on silver trays.

—LEWIS H. LAPHAM, IN THE BOOK *MONEY AND CLASS IN AMERICA: NOTES AND OBSERVATIONS ON OUR CIVIL RELIGION*

■ Money also makes it easier to account for the value of things. By reducing the value of things to dollars and cents (or yen or marks or pesos or whatever), we can more easily compare. Without it, our accounting gets pretty weird: one dozen eggs equals one bushel of wheat equals two steaks equals one sixteenth of a automobile transmission equals one senior manager's memo.

"SMOKE 'EM IF YOU'VE GOT 'EM"—A RANDOM SAMPLE OF ALTERNATIVE FORMS OF CURRENCY THROUGH THE AGES

So you don't want to carry a transmission with you every time you go to the store? Well, you're in luck, for over time, currency has included many other (smaller, lighter) things:

■ Going back a few thousand years, skins appear to have served as one of the earliest forms of currency. This was certainly true for the Inuit of Alaska and the Zulu and Kaffir of Africa. Interestingly, as people learned to domesticate animals, the livestock instead of the skins became the medium of exchange. This was also true in Rome, where 10 sheep, for example, might be considered a fair exchange for one ox. This concept of critters as currency appears in even ancient literature. For instance, in the *Iliad*, one finds sets of armor being valued relative to the number of oxen they will fetch.

■ If we look back at early Australians, we see that early trading for them was between groups or tribes, not individuals. For instance, the stone used to make hatchet heads would be carried hundreds of miles by the people of one tribe and exchanged for the valued goods or raw materials that were produced by other tribes or were indigenous to the other tribes' region.

■ Corn was used as a medium of exchange in Norway. Other food products that have served as currency are olive oil, coconuts, and tea. Even salt was once used as a form of currency in Mexico.

■ Tobacco was used as a medium of exchange in the early North American colonies.

■ In British Columbia, strings of haiqua shells served two purposes: jewelry and items to be exchanged for other goods. For instance, a string of shells of passable quality might be considered

equal in value to one beaver skin. The Fijians once used whale teeth for trade, and some South Seas tribes used red feathers.
■ Soldiers during World War II often played poker for cigarettes.

THE GOLD STANDARD*

In the good old days (a.k.a. the good gold days), people would travel around with bags of gold hidden in their pockets or bags or tied to their belts at the waist. This arrangement made life a bit inconvenient because every time you wanted to trade some gold for something else, the gold would have to be weighed and assessed for purity. Now, wouldn't that just thrill everyone standing behind you in the "cash only—six items or less" line at your local supermarket?

To solve the problem, along came a guy who called himself a "goldsmith." He would weigh your gold, assess its purity, and then hang onto it for you for safekeeping. In exchange for your gold, he would give you a receipt. Well, it didn't take folks long to figure out that it was a lot easier to carry those receipts with them than it was to go to the goldsmith to get gold and then haul the actual gold around, so people started accepting goldsmith receipts in trade for goods and services.

Voilà! The first paper currency was born.

Next, the goldsmiths realized that while they had everyone's gold in storage, hardly anyone ever came to trade their receipts for the gold itself. Hmmm. What a waste. All that gold was sitting there doing nothing.

One bright goldsmith had a great idea: If hardly anyone ever

---

* So, what is the gold standard? Actually, a better question would be this: What *was* the gold standard? That's because we don't have one anymore.

As the name implies, when a country's monetary policy is based on a gold standard, it means that somewhere in a vault is a dollar's worth of gold for every dollar in your pocket. It also means that you should be able to go to where that vault is located and trade your paper dollar for a dollar's worth of gold at any time you wish.

Of course, if you stop for a moment and think about it, this gold standard thing has some problems.

For instance, if there is no more gold being found, then there is no more money being created; conversely, if a lot of gold is found, a lot of money is created overnight. The latter problem is why inflation was so dramatic in the gold rush days in California. The former problem is what finally caused the whole gold standard thing to crumble. You see, in the late years of the nineteenth century, both the European nations and the United States operated on the gold standard. From 1870 until the outbreak of World War I, the English pound was the preferred currency of international trade, although it came to redeem their receipts for their gold, that meant that he could give out some of the gold to other people who were willing to take it now and pay it back, plus interest, later.

It goes something like this. Joe Goldsmith gives a receipt to Bob, who deposits a pound of gold with Joe. Jane comes to Joe Goldsmith and says, "Hey, Joe, let me use some of that gold you have there. Yeah, the stuff Bob left. I'll pay you back before Bob even notices, and even give you a little extra for your trouble. In fact, don't even bother giving me the gold; just give me one of those receipts. After all, those things are as good as gold!"

So, Joe gives Jane a receipt. Voilà! The interest-bearing loan is born.

Now, think about it. After Joe and Jane conduct their little transaction, the town has two receipts out there, each being backed up by the same gold—Bob's gold—in Joe's shop. You ask, "Isn't that called double-dipping?" Nope. It's called the fractional reserve system. And to this day, it's the way banks "create" money. Of course, these days, its all quite sophisticated, with electronic transfers and all, but the principle is the same. Banks pay the people who deposit money a small amount of interest and then lend the money at a higher rate of interest. The spread between the higher and lower rates is what the bank gets to keep. And, if this spread—plus other fees the bank gets paid—is more than the bank pays for buildings and tellers and ATM machines and so on, then the bank makes a profit.

Simple, right?

---

didn't really matter whose money you used as long as it was one tied into the value of gold.

However, with the outbreak of World War I, England needed to buy a bunch of stuff—like machine guns and soldier rations—and this gold standard thing was beginning to get in the way. If you close your eyes, you can almost hear the conversation:

"Excuse me, Mr. Bank of England, do you really have a piece of gold in your vault to support this purchase you're making here?"

"Shut up! We're at war! Take this paper currency. We'll sort out the gold thing after we win."

Well, that all seemed fine as a stopgap emergency measure. But after 40 years of world war and economic depression and world war again, the whole gold standard thing was kind of in shambles.

What was a beleaguered economic system to do? Call a conference, of course! (See "Taking a Walk through Bretton Woods," page 68.)

Well, yes and no. Just when you thought you were really getting a handle on Monetary Economics 101, we have to tell you that it's slightly more complicated. You see, banks don't just create money. When you get a bunch of banks together, each taking deposits and making loans like we described, then the banks actually multiply the amount of money in the economy.

DON'T PUT YOUR MONEY UNDER YOUR MATTRESS

You may be thinking, *Yeah, but what happens if Bob shows up at Joe's bank and wants his million? In fact, what if everyone who's made deposits shows up on the same day and wants his or her cash?*

Well, if that happens, the bank has a big problem. Remember Jimmy Stewart in the movie *It's a Wonderful Life*? He had this problem. It's called a run on the bank and can result when people panic and begin to worry that everyone else might go to the bank first and take all the money and the bank will close and leave them empty-handed.

Odds are, though, this will never happen to you—for two reasons. First, the banks keep enough cash on hand to handle most normal—that is, nonpanicky—situations. In fact, the government regulates banks and requires them to keep enough on hand for most normal situations. Second, the government has a deposit insurance program in place. The main point of the insurance program is that it reduces panic, and less panic means fewer runs on banks, which means fewer panic-induced bank failures. Which means your money is probably pretty safe right where it is down at the bank, even though it's not really there.

STOP THE PRESSES!

If only you were a bank . . . then you too could make money with the multiplier effect. Now that we know all that we know about banks and deposits and double-dipping, it's time to learn about triple-dipping, quadruple-dipping, and on and on and on. It works like this:

- You deposit $100 in your bank, the United Bank of Banking. According to the law, your bank must keep at least 20% of all deposits on reserve. So, thanks to your deposit, the bank can now lend $80, or we might say that the bank has just created

$80 on which it will now collect interest.

- Now Jane goes to the same bank, the United Bank of Banking, and borrows $80. She uses it to pay her landlord, Frank.

- Frank deposits the check for $80 with his bank, First Federal Bank.

- According to the law, of course, First Federal must keep at least 20% (or $16) of all deposits in reserve. So, thanks to Frank's deposit, the bank can now lend $64:

$80 × 20% = $16; $80 − $16 = $64

- Steve goes to First Federal and borrows $64, then uses the money to buy a pair of shoes at Kmart.

- Kmart deposits the $64 in its bank, the Big Bank of Borneo.

- Of course, Big Bank must keep at least 20% of all deposits in reserve, but that still leaves $51.20 of Kmart's deposit that the bank can lend to someone else:

"GIVE ME A DOLLAR'S WORTH"

Isn't it strange? Even though most of the colonists in the new United States were from England, the leaders of the new nation decided to name their federal currency the dollar, after the Spanish dollar instead of after the English pound of their homeland. Turns out it wasn't a strange choice at all . . . but one that merely made good economic sense. You see, in the early days of the United States, the balance of trade was such that Americans bought a lot more stuff from England than they sold to Britishers, but they sold a lot more stuff to Spain than they bought from the Spanish. So there were always lots of dollars floating around, but what few pounds there were were always being sent back to England to pay for merchandise. Therefore, it made a lot more sense to name the new currency after the same money that was already heavily in circulation.

$64 × 20% = $12.80; $64 − $12.80 = $51.20

- Rick comes along and borrows $51.20 from Big Bank and uses the money to buy his girlfriend dinner. Nick's Café Américan deposits the $51.20 into its bank, Casa Blanca Savings & Loan.

- Casa Blanca Savings & Loan, of course, must keep 20% of all deposits on reserve, but that still leaves the bank $40.96 that it can lend to someone else:

$51.20 × 20% = $10.94; $51.20 − 10.94 = $40.96

- Yes, you guessed it. Sandy walks into Casa Blanca Savings & Loan and borrows $40.96 and . . . well, how far do you want to take this? The bottom line is that with your deposit of $100, lots of banks get to create a lot of money (almost $400, if you play it out far enough) and make money off the money (in the form of interest paid on the loans), to boot.

Not bad, huh?

Of course, when a bank miscalculates how much it will need in its reserves and then comes up short, there's only one place to go to get the needed cash: The bank has to borrow it from someone else, like the Federal Reserve. We'll talk more about the Fed later.

TAKING A WALK THROUGH BRETTON WOODS

At the end of World War II, leaders of 44 countries from around the world met with John Maynard Keynes in Bretton Woods, New Hampshire, to try to bring order to the prevailing international chaos caused by the Great Depression, two world wars, and the end of the gold standard.

There were two major breakthroughs as a result of the Bretton Woods Conference:

"DO AS I SAY, AND DO AS I DO"

The law that denied citizens the right to own gold was repealed in 1975. According to economist John Kenneth Galbraith, the movement to repeal the law was headed by Senator James L. Buckley, brother of the famous conservative commentator William F. Buckley Jr. As Galbraith tells it, on the day Congress passed the repeal, Senator Buckley was one of the first in line at his bank to buy gold.

- The International Monetary Fund (IMF) was set up to act as a sort of international Federal Reserve. It was formed to foster international trade and help different countries trade their currencies for the currencies of other nations. Among other things, the IMF was to oversee a system in which the U.S. dollar was tied to gold and everything else was tied to the dollar.

- The World Bank was born. The goal was to create an international banking institution that would first make long-term loans to countries that were in the need of funds for reconstruction due to damage from the just-ended second world war and also offer Third World countries long-term loans for suitable development projects.

PURCHASING POWER OF A DOLLAR, 1792–1999

Ever get the feeling that no matter how much you make, it's never enough, even if you make more and more every year? (See graph on page 70.)

VALUE OF GOLD, 1792–1998

Good thing gold is nature's most malleable metal—its value takes a beating over time, then bounces back. (See graph on page 71.)

WHAT PRICE PIRACY?

It seems like just yesterday you could go to almost any bank you wanted and use your ATM card to get cash for free, or darn near free. Then, one day, that free service suddenly cost somewhere between $1.50 and $5.00.

If you're like us, these fees cheese you off. We liked the convenience of being able to get cash almost anywhere in the world, 24 hours a day, without having to wait for the bank to open or ever having to wait in line. And just in case we haven't made the point yet, we really liked it when it was free.

When banks started charging fees (and double fees—one from the host bank and one from your own bank), we ranted and raved about it. (This is especially true of your cheapskate author.) Then we realized something: It's just another example of supply and demand.

When you go to an ATM and agree to pay the fee (or double fee) to get some cash, you are in essence saying you value the service and convenience of that ATM at least as much as the cost of the fee. Meanwhile, obviously, enough other people value the service and convenience to pay the fees, because you see ATM machines sprouting up almost everywhere.

If you find, in spite of reading this brief analysis, that you are still ticked off about the fees, we suggest you try looking at ATMs in a different light. Instead of regarding them as money machines, think of them as convenience machines instead. There are lots of

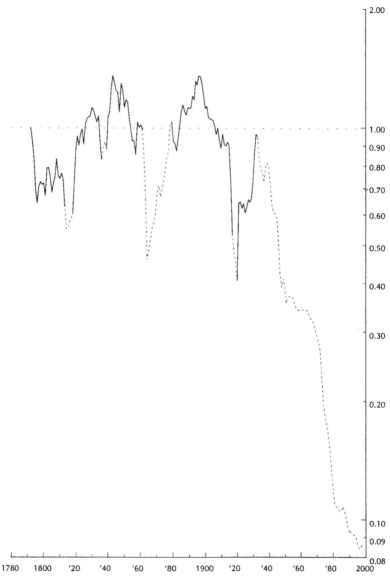

Calculated from the Bureau of Labor Statistics' Wholesale Price Index. Broken portions of the graph illustrate time periods when the dollar could not be redeemed for gold at a fixed rate.

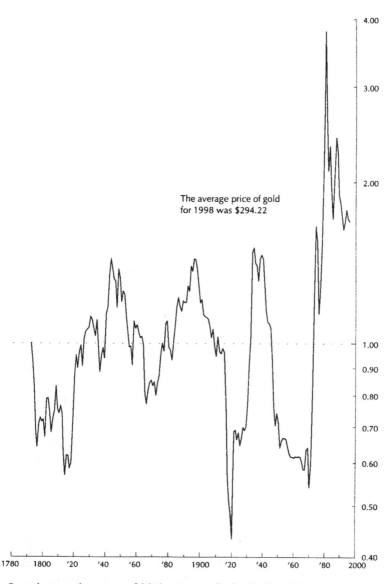

The average price of gold
for 1998 was $294.22

From the annual averages of (1) the Bureau of Labor Statistics' Wholesale Price
Index and (2) the exchange ratio of dollars and gold.

ways you can get cash for free: You can go to the bank, cash a check at the supermarket, or make a purchase with your debit card and get cash back.

However, we think you'll agree that going to the nearest ATM machine is a heck of a lot more convenient. (Similarly, it is often a lot easier to go to a convenience store to pick a few items than it is to go to a supermarket, yet no one is ever surprised or upset to find that the price of bread or soap or ice cream is higher there.)

Now, the question becomes this: Are you willing to pay a couple of bucks for convenience? If so, go to the ATM. If not, use an alternative—albeit less convenient—method to land cash without a fee. (By the way, we would be remiss if we didn't point out that these infernal fees are the perfect example of a product that had to be given away at first to create initial demand [like our earlier examples of Xerox machines and cell phones]. It is also a perfect case study for the concept of elasticity. Some people think nothing of spending a couple of dollars for the convenience of getting cash. Their demand for convenience is elastic. The question is, how elastic? Will they pay $5 to get money? $7? $10? Others, who have completely inelastic demand, would never spend a cent of their hard-earned money on convenient cash; they go out of their way to find free alternatives to the robber-baron ATMs.)

"WELCOME TO FANTASY ISLAND"

Given the law of supply and demand, you know that one day a bank will come along that figures out how to cash in on ATM-fee outrage in a way that also serves its own best interest.

A bank's self-interest can be advanced by getting more customers. And to do that, some bank will figure that it can attract hordes of new customers and new deposits by loudly and publicly proclaiming that not only does it refuse to charge its customers ATM fees but it also will reimburse them for any fees levied by other banks. Of course, those of us who hate the fees will fantasize that people will flock to this bank, leaving the other banks stunned by the giant sucking sound of their money being withdrawn from their vaults. As the fantasy continues, other banks quickly figure out what has happened and they, too, begin offering ATM fee–free banking.

And so on. And ridiculous double-dipping ATM fees will be a thing of the past. (But, alas, there are too many ATM customers with elastic demand for convenience for this fantasy to ever come true.) However, it appears that there might be enough of us ATM-fee haters (a.k.a. customers with inelastic demand) to have some impact on the marketplace.

For instance, regional bank LBA Savings Bank in Louisiana realized it just couldn't compete with the big banks when it came to building an ATM network. So, its officers figured, why bother trying? Instead, they devised a plan to keep their existing customers happy and win hordes of new customers from those same big banks. Instead of charging customers when they use another bank's ATM, LBA began a policy of paying their customers' ATM fees at "foreign" banks instead. Yes, that's right: If you are a customer of LBA and you use another bank's ATM, LBA will pay you $1.50.

Talk about doing what serves your own best self-interest: LBA's customers can go to any ATM anytime they like, scot-free, which is great for them and great for LBA, who has amassed tremendous publicity, customer loyalty, and new clients.

Meanwhile, at KeyBank in Cleveland, you're charged $1.50 to see a live teller . . . but every time you use an ATM to do your banking, KeyBank will express its gratitude by crediting your account with a quarter.

THE LIFE SPAN OF ALAN GREENSPAN: REVEALING HIDDEN MYSTERIES BEHIND THE FEDERAL RESERVE BANK

WHAT IS THE FEDERAL RESERVE?

The Federal Reserve is a sort of central bank for the entire United States. It is governed by a seven-member board of governors, each of which is appointed by the president of the United States for a 14-year term. It is the governors' job to make monetary decisions that will promote the well-being of the economy as a whole.

Well, that's the official line, anyway. But a conflict of interest might be said to exist because the Fed is actually owned by its own member banks. It doesn't necessarily follow that what is good for banks is good for you or the national economy. For instance, you may want the Fed to lower interest rates so you can refinance your house and save a bundle of money every month. On the other hand, if the Fed does as you wish and lowers rates, this action contributes to inflation, which results in uncertainty in the economy, which causes market volatility, so you're going to pay for it anyway. So the Fed sees itself as trying to make the best choices for the economy at large.

WHERE IS THE FED?

There are actually twelve branches of the Federal Reserve. The main branch is in New York City and the remaining 11 are in Boston, Philadelphia, Richmond (Virginia), Cleveland, Atlanta, St. Louis, Dallas, Chicago, Kansas City, Minneapolis, and San Francisco.

Can you open an account with the Fed? Not unless you're the owner of a bank yourself. You see, the Fed is sort of a banker's bank. It plays the same role for banks that your bank plays for you. You deposit money at your bank; your bank deposits money at the Fed. You borrow money from your bank; your bank borrows money from the Fed. You use your ATM card to get cash at your bank; your bank . . . well, okay, let's not get carried away here. However, there are many similarities in the two relationships. For instance, when you write a check on your bank in Kalamazoo, Michigan, and then send it to a friend who deposits it in a bank in Boston, it is the Fed that squares up the accounts by drawing on the reserves of your bank and crediting the reserves of your friend's bank.

DOES THE FED DO MORE THAN SERVE AS A BANK FOR BANKERS?

The Fed influences the availability of money in the economy. It does this in three ways.

First, its board of governors sets the rate at which member banks can borrow money. When this rate goes down, so do the interest rates at which you can borrow. And vice versa. And, remember, the more people borrow, the more money is multiplied. (This is a bit oversimplified, we admit, but you get the idea.) Second, it buys and sells government bonds from banks. When the Fed buys these bonds from a bank, it does so by giving the bank more cash—and we now know what banks do with cash: They multiply it! Third, the Fed sets the amount of reserves each bank must keep.

The Fed doesn't mess with this reserve policy very much, but you can see how it could affect the amount of money in the system if it changed: If banks needed to keep 50% of every deposit in the vault instead of, say, 10%, they'd have a lot less to lend and there'd be a lot less money created by the multiplier effect.

WHY DO WE NEED A FED?

Do we really need a Fed? Well, there are those who say we don't. Some say that if there is going to be a governing body overseeing our national monetary policy, then that governing body ought to at least be elected or appointed by Congress or something. Otherwise, Congress is being held responsible, in part, for the actions of people over whom they have no control. Supporters of the Fed say that if we are to have a panel with this much control over our monetary policy, then the panel must be free of political pressure. After all, if the members of the Fed had to run for reelection every two or four or six years, then the decisions they made might be colored by the short-term need to please voters instead of by what would be best for the national economy in the long run. There is validity to both views.

HOW TO READ TEA LEAVES AND DEPOSIT SLIPS

If a bank has to keep some percentage of its deposits at the Fed on reserve and if money flows in and out of the bank every day—as money is deposited, loans are paid, checks are written, funds are withdrawn, and money is lent—how can the bank make sure, on any given day, that the reserve requirement will be met?

A. Call the Psychic Bankers' Network.

B. Rely on the law of averages. Given the number of clients a bank has making and withdrawing money, it's a pretty safe bet that after all is said and done at the end of the day, the bank will have about as much on deposit as it did when the day began.

C. Borrow from the Fed or another bank. If the law of averages lets the bank down and the bank doesn't have enough money to meet the Fed's reserve requirements at the end of the day, it can always borrow money from the Fed itself to make up the difference. Nifty, huh? Sort of like borrowing money from Visa to pay off American Express. Which, by the way, lots of people do.

Answer: These days, it's a combination of B and C. Back in the '80s, before the S&L crisis was made public, bankers relied a little more heavily on A.

WHERE DOES ALAN GREENSPAN FIT IN?

When this book went to press, Greenspan was the chairman of the Federal Reserve Board. Because while he's been in office he has had more control over the monetary policy of the United States than anyone else, some people have considered him to be the most powerful man in the world. President Ronald Reagan offered him the chairmanship of the Fed in 1987. President George H. W. Bush asked him to stay for a second four-year term in 1992, and President Bill Clinton asked him to stay on for a third four-year term in 1996. Although Alan Greenspan may no longer be the head of the Fed by the time you read this, his influence will still be felt.

At the time this book was published, Alan Greenspan had been the chairman of the Fed for 12 years. What a lucky guy. He took the job in August 1987, just two months before the October crash that is now affectionately remembered as Black Monday.

Greenspan responded then as he has responded to everything that has come at him since—calmly. Perhaps he learned to keep his cool while in college—in fact, he was a music major and studied music at one of the best music schools in the country, the Juilliard School in New York City. As a jazz saxophonist, he toured the country with a swing band, then went back to school to earn a bachelor's degree and then a master's degree from New York University. And you might think that the most powerful man in the world in the world of economics and finance would naturally have a doctorate as well.

Well, he does. But he certainly didn't come by it naturally. Or quickly. In fact, he didn't get his doctorate until he was already the chairman of the Council of Economic Advisors under President Gerald Ford, more than 25 years after he completed his master's degree. And, in fact, New York University awarded him the doctorate without ever requiring him to complete his dissertation.

WHAT'S IT TAKE TO BE CHAIRPERSON OF THE FED?

Who better to ask about the qualifications for leading the Fed than poet and former accounting teacher Allan Marcus:

> The penguin Pierpoint
> The president did appoint,

And Congress so anoint,
To publicly serve
As the head bird
Of the Federal Reserve.

With his cold, icy heart,
Pierpoint was perfect
For this monetary part.
Reserved in his
Stuffed shirt and bow tie,
To Congress, Pierpoint
Would intricately testify,
While never knowingly lie.

Through the use of
Interest rates,
The economy
He could manipulate.

If our fiscal policy
Was too sedate,
His precious touch
Had better not
Overinvigorate.

Pierpoint was also
A sweet-toothed dandy.
It was his idea to convert
The money supply
To candy.

Savings no longer
Would be a chore
As we stockpiled
Our chocolate hoard.

When the economy required an
Interest rate kicker,
It could be enticed
With Snickers.

And if fiscally
We got too hot,
The Fed resolved,
Our candy money supply
Easily could be dissolved.

WHICH CAME FIRST — THE CHICKEN OR THE EGG?

A chicken is just an egg's way of making more eggs so . . . the egg. By the way, mankind is just pig iron's way of making more pig iron, so obviously, the pig iron came first.

— PAUL ANTHONY SAMUELSON, WINNER OF THE 1970 NOBEL PRIZE FOR ECONOMICS

When Alan Greenspan, chief economist of the world, decided to make a proposal of marriage at age 70 to his longtime lady friend and prominent Washington, D.C., TV reporter Andrea Mitchell, she didn't have a clue as to what he was talking about.

Even when he tried to propose a second time, she later told a friend, she "just didn't get it."

This is a common reaction if you're listening to an economist speak. Your head may start to spin in that way that implies you're either not getting enough oxygen or you're trying to follow the logic of someone who is seemingly not making any sense.

As was the case with Alan Greenspan and Andrea Mitchell, it might be the economist—not the economics—that is throwing you off.

DECIPHERING OTHER FEDMEISTERS

For his book *Secrets of the Temple: How the Federal Reserve Runs the Country,* William Greider interviewed all the major players in the Federal Reserve System. A *New York Times* bestseller and described by *The Nation* magazine as "maybe the most important political book of the decade" (1980s), it is an extremely helpful resource for understanding the mystery of monetary economics.

GETTING SOAKED WITH THE HEAD OF THE FED AND THE PREZ

The president of the United States and the head of the Federal Reserve in a bathtub together?

Not likely.

Which is ironic, since this unusual (if not repugnant) image is the start of the best way to begin to understand the relationship among the Fed, the U.S. government, and the U.S. economy.

For the sake of conversation, let's just say the head of the Fed and the prez are in a very special tub. It's big enough to hold two leaders comfortably without them ever needing to touch (because we're a family kind of book, after all).

Both have a faucet and a drain. Regardless of who turns on the faucet, the act represents the flow of money. When the president opens his faucet, government spending comes shooting out. When the head of the Fed opens his faucet, out flows Fed policy designed to stimulate the economy and lower interest rates. The president's drain represents taxes. The head of the Fed's drain represents savings. The level of water in the tub represents jobs. When the tub is full you've got full employment; drain it a bit and you get some degree of unemployment. The water level also represents the state of the economy as a whole. When the tub is full, the economy is operating at its peak. If the economy is underperforming, you can judge the state of things by looking at how far below the lip of the tub the water level has dropped.

Both of our economic heavyweights are trying to control the economy using all of the tools (a faucet and a drain) at their disposal. Of course, things would probably work better if they coordinated their efforts and worked together. Unfortunately, they don't always have the same goal in mind.

The beauty of this bathtub analogy is that it makes clear that no matter how complicated you (assuming the "you" we're talking about is the president of the United States or the chairman of the Fed) think the problems of the economy are, you only have four options (turn on your faucet, shut off your faucet, open your drain, close your drain) open to you in order to clear those problems up.

You might find it interesting to know that when the Fed takes some action to impact the economy, it's called monetary policy because any action it takes will affect the price and supply of money within the economy. On the other hand, when the president takes some action to impact the economy, it's called fiscal policy. *Fiscal,* as in finances—because when the president monkeys with the economy he is really monkeying with the nation's budget. After all, a budget is simply an estimate of what you will spend and receive in a given period. When the president raises or lowers taxes, he is changing how much the nation will receive in revenue. An increase or decrease in government spending is a change in what the nation will spend.

"Okay," you say, "but let's get back to our bathtub: If solving economic problems is as simple as taking a bath, why do we keep having so many problems?"

This is an excellent question. And there are lots of good answers. We'll give you a sample of some of our favorites.

1. One reason economic problems defy simple solutions is that we don't always know how much of a good thing we should use. In other words, the head of the Fed may know that lowering interest rates is called for by a high unemployment situation. So he turns on his faucet to stimulate the economy and create jobs. But how far should he open the faucet? And how long should he leave the water running?

The truth is, we don't always know exactly how high we should let the water level get, how much water we should let out of the faucet, and how much water we should let escape down the drain. If the president doesn't open the faucet far enough, it won't make much difference. All the water he adds will just flow down his drain or the drain of the Fed head. And if he adds too much water? He overprimes the economy, causes full employment, and water spills all over the floor.

The same issues apply to taxes. And to government spending. Meanwhile, when it comes to taxes and spending, there is also the little question of who gets taxed and what we should spend the tax revenue on. Increasing taxes as a policy prescription may sound fine in principle . . . as long as we're not the ones being taxed. Spending sounds wonderful if you spend it on my son's school, my favorite national park, and the public transit system near where I live . . . but not if you're planning to spend it on Cruise missiles made 3,000 miles from where I live, or on a subsidy for a large nuclear power plant in my backyard.

2. Economic problems defy simple solutions because policies must be coordinated to have the desired effect. And this coordination is often difficult to achieve.

Let's return to our bathtub analogy. Here are two guys, each with his own faucet and his own drain. A stable and healthy economy, of course, is always their goal. The economy is stable when the water level remains constant, going neither up nor down; it's healthy when the water level is somewhere near the top of the tub.

For the sake of this example, let's say the tub is about 90% full and holding. Everybody knows that 90%—"Hey, that's a pretty healthy economy!" But you're the president, and you're running for reelection. And you know that if you could get that tub up to about 95% full, you'd be a shoo-in.

So let's suppose the prez cranks up his faucet and closes his drain . . . trying to raise the water level. And suppose that, at the same time, the Fed chairperson is thinking that a tub (or economy) at 90% is a little too high; the danger of full employment is looming and would surely bring on a bad case of inflation. So he cuts off *his* faucet and opens *his* drain . . . trying to lower the water level.

Voilà! Poor coordination.

In fact, this working at cross-purposes is exactly what happened in the Great Depression. With macroeconomics in its infancy, the monetary authorities didn't understand they needed to loosen the reins on the availability of money. Instead, they held money tight . . . so all the stimulating policies of the New Deal were being offset by other policies.

3. Finally, governmental policies and the Fed aren't the only things affecting the behavior of the economy. In fact, as the modern economy grows larger and larger and more global, many people argue that individual governments' ability to influence the economy is becoming less and less significant. In other words, in addi-

tion to the prez and the Fed chairperson turning faucets and drains on and off, there are consumers and businesses and foreign governments and foreign consumers and foreign businesses, each with their own faucets and drains! In fact, it's like one giant tub full of loosely coordinated individuals all trying to set faucets and drains to suit themselves. From this perspective, it's fairly miraculous that we get the water level as close to full as often as we do!

RUB-A-DUB-DUB . . . TWO BELTWAY INSIDERS IN A TUB

Enough of this conceptual talk. Let's put our pair of bathing beauties to work on the two most common economic problems— inflation and unemployment—of our times.

MEET THE "EVIL TWINS" OF ECONOMICS

As we all know, inflation is bad. And unemployment is bad. The problem is, the solution for one can be the cause of the other.

Take unemployment. The solution, of course, is to create jobs and raise the level of water in that tub. The prez can cure unemployment by closing his drain (cutting taxes) or turning the water on higher (spending more government dough). The head of the Fed can open his faucet or close his drain, in both cases with the intention of lowering interest rates and stimulating investment.

If the prez and the Fed head are successful, there will be money coursing through the economy and jobs aplenty.

Which is a problem. Because, as we discussed earlier, full employment causes inflation.

Now, let's play this backward like an old home movie: You've just solved the unemployment problem. See how easy it was! But what happens if you do such a good job that more jobs are created than there are people around to fill them?

The answer is you get water spilling over the side of the tub and all over the floor. It rots the linoleum, then the floorboards, and then the floor itself.

It turns out that the creation of too many jobs has a similar effect. Only this time, we call the result inflation instead of rot.

Before inflation can set in, however, you often experience a phenomenon called full employment. If you have a job, full employment sounds great because it means employers are so desperate for good help that they'll do almost anything to get you to work for them. They'll pay more, reduce hours, increase vacation time, give large bonuses, install a gym . . . whatever it takes.

The problem is, where a worker may see a full tub, an economist tends to see a tub about to overflow.

It's another reason economists get labeled "dismal."

Everyone's dancing naked in the tub, having a great old full-employment kind of time, and the economist is focused on that running faucet and the fact that the water is about to go cascading over the edge.

Full employment means there's the same amount of jobs as there are qualified people to take them. If the faucet keeps running (i.e., if the economy keeps demanding more and more investment and consumer goods), businesses will want even more employees than there are qualified ones available. The result? Everyone will have to be paid more to stay with the jobs they have (or they'll leave to go to better-paying jobs somewhere else, only to be lured away by yet another company with a job offer that comes with another wage increase attached). If everyone is making oodles more money, but the same amount of stuff is getting made overall, the price of everything will increase by a correspondingly oodlesome amount. Pretty soon, you've got a vicious cycle. No matter where you look—at wages, the price of food, the price of cars, the price of housing, the price of shoelaces—prices just keep going up, up, up.

And when that happens, you've got a textbook example of inflation.

TEXTBOOK DEFINITION OF INFLATION

An increase in the general level of prices in an economy that is sustained over time. . . . Inflation reduces the purchasing power of money . . . (and) creates uncertainty and obstacles to future transactions.

—THE HARPERCOLLINS *DICTIONARY OF ECONOMICS*

We will add to this definition by pointing out that there are actually two types of inflation: demand-pull inflation, which comes from too much total spending, and cost-push inflation, which happens when businesses continue to raise their prices because their own costs continue to rise. Meanwhile, if you want to get a grip on just how fast those prices are rising, you can always apply the rule of 70, which is a handy trick for figuring out how fast—in years—current prices will double. To apply the rule of 70, simply divide 70 by your current rate of inflation.

Now, for those people who are really paying close attention, a question usually arises about this inflation thing, and it goes something like this: If everybody's wages are rising by the same amount that prices are rising, what's the problem?

The answer is twofold.

First, not everybody's wages rise during inflationary times. For instance, some people, such as retirees who receive pensions or other retirement benefits, live on fixed incomes. In times of inflation, when you and everyone else with a job gets a raise, they have to continue to live on the same amount as before.

Second, high inflation causes a lot of uncertainty about the future. Whether we're talking about you and your paycheck or the CEO of the company you work for or the guy who owns the little market around the corner from your house, it's one thing to expect a 3% rise in prices and find out that you were wrong when prices actually rise 4%. A 1% difference will be just cause for a little belt-tightening, but it won't be the end of the world. But if prices are expected to rise 15% and they actually go up 20%, that's a difference that could really cause some serious problems. By definition, high inflation occurs when prices are going up faster than anyone expects—and when that happens, everyone loses confidence in the economy. People begin spending a lot of time and energy figuring out how to protect their earnings against inflation rather than buying stuff. At the same time, companies are also working overtime to figure out how to protect their earnings against inflation instead of working to

GOOD BATHTUB READING

Arthur M. Okun served as the chairman of the Council of Economic Advisors in the Lyndon Johnson administration. In his book *Equality and Efficiency, the Big Tradeoff,* he laid out the essential issues of political economy in four very readable chapters: Rights and Dollars, The Case for the Market, Equality of Income and Opportunity, and Increasing Equality in an Efficient Economy. The book is a gem and is not as widely read by economists (or the public) as it should be.

make new and better products to meet people's needs. The result: People spend less, so companies produce less, and when companies produce less they need fewer workers so they lay people off . . . so people with jobs get more nervous and spend less and people who have been laid off spend even less than that, so companies produce even less . . . and so on. In fact, the overflowing tub is a good analogy because persistent inflation will eat away at the very foundation of a sound economy the same way water from an overflowing bathtub will eventually begin to rot the bathroom linoleum, the floorboards, and the floor itself.

WHY YOU'D HATE INFLATION IF YOU WERE A BANKER

When interest rates are low, everyone loves the bank. We ecstatically refinance our homes and consolidate our debts to make home improvements. We buy boats and new cars. And why not? The price of money is cheap, so we all walk around feeling the good love groove about our bank. And those banks are sending love vibes right back. Then that ugly old inflation comes around. Suddenly, the bank has a problem. Money isn't buying what it used to . . . including more money. If the interest the bank is collecting on an outstanding loan is less than the current rate of inflation, then it's losing money on the loan. That's easy to understand, isn't it? If you lend your best friend a hundred dollars today, payable in a year, at 5% interest, in a year you will have made five bucks. Or, in more relative terms, you figured you'd be able to buy 5% more stuff after your best friend paid you back. But that's only true in a world with no inflation. So factor that in. Let's say you make the loan—a hundred dollars today, payable in a year, at 5% interest. There's 5% inflation over the course of that year. How much more stuff can you buy with that $105 than you could have with the $100 a year earlier? The answer is, not a single stick of gum. The money you made in interest was completely gobbled up by the inflation monster. And what if you had made the same deal with your friend a year ago and there was 7% inflation? Unfortunately, you would find that you could buy less today with the money your friend repaid you than you could have with your initial hundred a year ago.

Now you can see why this is such a problem for banks. They lent out their money with the intention of making money, but instead they're actually losing money on any outstanding loans written for a rate of interest below the rate of inflation.

And that, as we all know, ain't good business.

WHO'S WHO AMONG THE UNEMPLOYED

- The *frictionally unemployed* are those who quit a job voluntarily and will be taking another shortly, and those who are seasonally unemployed (such as department-store Santa Clauses and beach lifeguards).
- The *structurally unemployed* lose their jobs when the economy itself changes. A secretary who has not learned to use a computer may become structurally unemployed, along with the steelworker who loses his job because so much steel is now made overseas.
- The *cyclically unemployed* are those who lose their jobs because the business cycle is in a lull and the economy is weak.

DEATH AND TAXES

It was Ben Franklin who once said, "... in this world, nothing is certain but death and taxes." No matter how much we may grumble about taxes, we guess we'd still prefer them over Ben's other alternative. Here's a primer on the different ways a government can collect its dough.

FLAT TAX

The flat tax is also known as a proportional tax. It works like this: if you make $10,000 a year, you pay 10% of it to the government as tax. If you make $50,000 a year, you pay 10% of it to the government as tax. If you make $100,000 a year, you pay 10% of it to the government as tax. And if you make $500,000 a year, you pay 10% of it to the government as tax. Are you beginning to see a pattern here?

REGRESSIVE TAX

Regressive taxes are those which, proportionally speaking, cost the poor more than they cost the rich. A good example? Sales tax. Let's say I go to the store and spend $100 on groceries and you go to the store and spend $100 on groceries. And let's just say we both pay $8 in taxes for those groceries. Couldn't you then also say that we were both taxed equally? The answer, according to some, is no, and here's why: If I make $50,000 per year and spend $100 on groceries and you earn $25,000 per year and spend $100, you have actually paid twice as much tax as I have, relative to our two incomes.

Some people have a slightly different take on the regressive tax, however. They say that the regressive tax is the only fair tax because it taxes you for only what you consume. Therefore, the rich will always pay more tax because they have more money to spend. So although the rich and the poor might both pay $8 tax on $100 worth of groceries, it is probably also true that the rich will spend a lot more than just the $100 on a week's worth of food. (Of course, as with all taxes, this argument comes with a loophole . . . if you're rich and don't like to pay taxes, you can avoid paying them by spending as little of your money as possible.)

PROGRESSIVE TAX

The progressive tax should sound familiar to you. It's the one the U.S. government uses today.

A progressive tax is one in which the rate at which a person is taxed increases as that person earns additional income. For instance, if you were single in 1998 and earned $25,350 or less, you paid income tax on 15% of your income. If you earned between $25,351 and $61,400, you paid 15% tax on the first $25,350 of income and 28% on the additional income. If you earned between $61,401 and $128,100, you paid 15% tax on the first $25,350 of income, 28% on the income between $25,351 and $61,401, and 31% on the additional income. If you earned between $128,101 and $278,450, you paid 15% tax on the first $25,350 of income, 28% on the income between $25,351 and $61,401, 36% on all the additional income. Finally, if you earned $278,4501 or more, you paid 15% tax on the first $25,350 of income, 28% on the income between $25,351 and $61,401, 36% on the income between $128,101 and $278,450, and 39.6% on all income above that.* You can begin to see the progressive nature of the tax. When you make more money, it puts you into another tax bracket and you pay a higher rate of tax on those dollars earned. You can also see why a flat tax ultimately benefits the rich. Whereas with a progressive tax they might end up paying as

---

* Please keep in mind that these figures only apply if you're single. Tax rates are different for married couples who file jointly, qualified widows and widowers, married couples who file separately, and heads of households. In addition, this information is in no way intended to be a substitute for the advice of a good accountant—or even of a bad one.

much as 39.6% of their income in taxes, under the flat or proportional tax they would never pay more than the fixed rate.

A SHORT HISTORY OF MISERY: TAXES THROUGHOUT THE AGES

Interestingly, good old civilized civilization as we know it brings along taxation as a matter of course.

Most people would agree that we need some form of taxation as a "fair" means of paying for government and its "fair" functions and programs. (You know, the stuff we all depend on: building roads, inspecting meat, bombing other countries—stuff like that.) Earlier civilizations were less fair, both in choosing taxable functions and in the way in which they went about figuring out how to pay for them:

- The Athenians, for instance, didn't need to tax the citizenry. They had plenty of money on hand from plundering publicly held mines and from conquering neighboring nations.

- In the Middle Ages, money ran uphill. Those on the low end of the food chain—peasants—paid rent to those who sat above them in the feudal hierarchy—landowners and lower-level gentry. Then the landowners and low-level gentry might pay a fee to those above them for the right to not serve in the military. Taxing, perhaps, but not quite taxation.

- If you were a king or queen during the Middle Ages, you were sitting pretty. You had a pretty good gig that worked a lot like what we call multilevel marketing today. You had a downline, and every time someone below you collected some rent, you got a piece of the pie. The only time this didn't provide you with sufficient income was when you were hit with an extraordinary expense, like hosting an epic war.

- Here's where taxation begins to resemble representation. You're the king or queen, you're having a great time fighting a war, you need extra dough. The only problem is, you need the help and support of your downline (a.k.a. landowners with vast holdings, other nobles). After all, who else is going to shake down the people on the street and collect that extra bit of cash? So you do what Amway and Excel and Shaklee and Mary Kay Cosmetics do today. You bring everyone in for a sales conference. You paint lots of bright-colored signs, play lots of loud music, teach the crowd a song and a cheer, then you send all on their way pumped up with enthusiasm, motivation, and inspiration. All in the name of taxation. However, things quickly evolved (or devolved, from the king's or queen's point of view). In no time at all, royals were no longer contacting the major landowners and nobles for help raising money so they could fight a war. Instead, the big cheeses were reduced to asking their subjects' permission. And thus was born the parliamentary form of government from the need for more taxes.

- Of course, people started to get used to having some say over what should be taxed and what shouldn't, so much so that when they were denied that right—as in the 13 colonies of the New World—they revolted with chants like "No taxation without representation!" and demonstrations like the Boston Tea Party and, later, the American war for independence.

Which brings us to the history of taxation in this country: The Founding Fathers knew that you couldn't run a country without some form of taxation or revenue. Since these were the same fellows who had just fought and won a war over unjust taxation, they wanted to make sure they didn't fall into the same trap. Yes, they needed money, to pay government employees and the militia, to run the post office, to build roads. Yes, they wanted to be fair. And it was James Madison who summed the situation up with two goals: (1) "to secure the object of revenue" but (2) to not be "oppressive to the constituents." Now, whether you think we have been successful at meeting Madison's goals probably depends on whether you are a Democrat or a Republican.

Taxation, in the early days of the United States, generally was levied in

> **THE SEVEN DEADLY TAXES**
>
> - Federal income tax
> - State income tax (if you live in one of 43 states)
> - Corporate income tax
> - Sales tax
> - Excise tax
> - Property tax
> - Payroll tax

the form of tariffs on certain luxury items, such as coffee and booze. Thus, the birth of the luxury tax—which would also qualify as a regressive tax, by the way. The United States enacted its first income tax during the Civil War. The law allowing the tax expired in 1872. In 1894, Congress passed another income tax law. Federal income tax as we know it became law in 1913, with the signing of the sixteenth amendment to the Constitution.

THE ONE BOOK I WOULD READ . . .

The book that has influenced me the most is a little bit obscure. It was a bestseller in the nineteenth century and it's called *Progress and Poverty* and was written by a man named Henry George. He was extremely famous a hundred years ago, and he's hardly heard of today. It was an economics book. It's very easy reading, given that it's a hundred years old and about economics. He was an autodidact; he was a self-trained thinker who ultimately ran for mayor of New York. He had a theory of the American economy that I think has lessons for today. In a nutshell, he thought that all problems are rooted in the ownership of land and he favored the elimination of all taxes other than a tax on land. He was sort of a nut, but what appeals to me about him is that he was a capitalist-socialist—he believed in the workings of the free market but he also believed in equality and he had a very interesting take on how those two goals can both be served.

—MICHAEL KINSLEY, POLITICAL COMMENTATOR

HOW TO WIN FRIENDS AND INFLUENCE PEOPLE WHILE AT AN AUDIT

You must remember this: A kiss is just a kiss and an audit is just an audit.* Even while you are sitting there in a chair at your local IRS office, with palms sweating, stomach churning, knees buckling, and heart pounding, it doesn't mean a darn thing unless someone makes a move to take things further.

---

* You must also remember this: An economist is an economist and an accountant is an accountant. Your accountant may fancy himself or herself an armchair economist, but no economist in his or her right mind ever thinks of himself or herself as an accountant. Which reminds us of this riddle: Do you know the difference between an economist and an accountant? The answer: An economist is an accountant without the charisma. Ba-dump-bump! And now to the point: Even though we offer this information on how to survive an audit as a public service, it's the kind of stuff you generally get from an accountant and not an economist.

How you handle a kiss is your own business. But here are our tips on how to make the best of a bad situation at the IRS:

- Don't try to win over the examiner or make him or her like you. After all, who needs a tax cop for a friend?
- Don't get mad. Don't get angry. Don't make threats. Don't bother reminding the examiner that you're the one who pays his or her salary. Don't threaten to call your congressional representative.
- Don't cheat on your taxes.
- Do be polite. But don't be too eager to please.
- Do keep answers brief, succinct, and to the point.
- Do answer all questions they ask, but don't volunteer any other information.

BETTER YET, HOW TO AVOID AN AUDIT ALTOGETHER

The good news is, you get better odds with the IRS than you do in Las Vegas, for it turns out that only 2% of all individual tax returns have been audited in recent years.

The bad news is, audits generally fall into two major categories: random and red flag. Random audits are just that . . . random. You didn't do anything wrong to trigger it and there's nothing you could have done to avoid it. Red-flag audits, on the other hand, are always triggered by something specific. All tax returns are run through a computer and the computer will flag all returns with high deductions or unusual (or suspicious) items. Those flagged returns are then reviewed by an agent, who decides whether an audit is warranted— so the best way to avoid an audit is to heed the following lists of do's and don'ts below, learn to think like an IRS agent and an IRS computer, and then avoid all things that would likely attract attention.

Do:

- Tell the truth.
- Save all necessary paperwork, even if you are telling a few little white lies.

- Avoid claiming itemized deductions that represent a large percentage of your annual income. If you do have a legitimate deduction that is substantial relative to your earned income, consider attaching a note or other documentation to the return explaining why you are claiming the deduction and why you think it is justified under the tax code.

- Avoid writing off large amounts of travel and entertainment expenses. However, if you think the amounts are large but justified, attach a note or other documentation telling the IRS why you feel that way.

- Live in Cincinnati. Don't live in L.A. It turns out that audits are assigned in regional IRS offices, and some offices do more auditing than others. Guess what? In 1996, L.A. taxpayers had the highest audit incident rate and Cincinnati taxpayers had the lowest.

Don't:

- Be stupid. Would you believe there are some people who lie to the IRS about how much they've made even when they know their employers have already sent the IRS their W-2s? If your income/salary/earnings/wages are on your employer's books, then the IRS already knows how much you made. So, we repeat: Don't be stupid.

- Tick off a coworker, employee, ex-lover, or ex-spouse so much that he or she turns you in to the IRS, which sometimes happens purely out of spite. (Regardless of why they do it, though, if the IRS nails you, the whistle-blower will be paid a reward.)

- Marry or do business with someone who is a likely IRS target. It turns out the agency likes to do what it calls related examinations, calling in for audits the friends, family, and associates of people whom it suspects of wrongdoing.

- Start a business, make a lot of money (in cash), and then file a Schedule C.

- Start a business, then fail; start another business, then fail; start another business, then fail; start another business, then fail— and expect the IRS to bail you out every time. Eventually, they'll lower the boom.

▪ Claim a home-office deduction. For some reason, the IRS is more suspicious of the at-home, self-employed type than of almost anyone else . . . mafia dons excluded.

ALWAYS LEAVE 'EM LAFFING—PART I

Has it been a long time since you had a good laugh over taxes? If so, we suggest you take a moment to consider the theory of economist Arthur B. Laffer and his Laffer curve.

According to Laffer, if tax rates were pushed too high, the end result would be that less taxes would be collected, instead of more taxes, which is the obvious intent.

Laffer based his theory on this premise: Anyone who has the willingness and means to start a new business or to invest in an existing business is doing so with the intent of making a healthy return on his or her money. If the tax rate gets too high, a healthy return will be reduced to a puny return . . . therefore, a tax rate that is too high will serve to stifle investment. And if investment is stifled, then less taxes will be collected.

Was Laffer right?

Well, as with many questions in economics, the answer is: It depends. In principle, it's probably true that at tax rates of close to 100% (that is, all money you make is taxed away), there will be no incentive to work, so there will be no income to tax, so tax revenue will be low. But, in the real world, tax rates are not near 100%. So, when the Reagan administration used the Laffer theory to justify cutting tax rates, most people in the know simply laughed. They knew that cutting tax rates would lower tax revenues, not raise them. Indeed, that's exactly what happened. Tax rates were cut, tax revenues declined, and we had the largest budget deficits ever recorded.

ALWAYS LEAVE 'EM LAFFING—PART II

When George H. W. Bush was running for the Republican presidential nomination in 1980 against Ronald Reagan, he referred to Reagan's economic proposals as "voodoo economics." A short time later, Bush found himself serving as Reagan's vice presidential running mate and then vice president . . . and his "voodoo" comment came back to haunt him. How could he support the economic policy of his boss after he had so vehemently dismissed it before, the press wanted to know. And George Bush did a silly thing: He denied he ever said it. "I didn't say it. I challenge anyone to find it" were his exact words. He was mortified when NBC accepted his challenge, found the "voodoo economics" quote on videotape, and played it over and over again for all the world to see.

AND LET'S NOT FORGET ABOUT ENTITLEMENTS . . .

It all started in the Great Depression, of course. No one had any money. No one had any food. No one had any nothing. Well, that's a rotten position to be in, whether the economy's at a dead halt or not.

Several states started their own unemployment programs and several others started their own old-age insurance plans. Then came the call to do both of these things on a national basis.

On one hand, the idea of this gave President Franklin D. Roosevelt a chill. Why, it almost sounded like socialism. On the other hand, given what people had just been through, the idea of unemployment and old-age insurance seemed to appeal to an awful lot of people. In 1934, Roosevelt weighed public opinion, took a deep breath, and appointed a committee to consider three different entitlement programs:

> **GET YOUR VOODOO DIRECT FROM THE SOURCE**
> If you ever wondered how Republicans think about economic issues and governmental participation in them, the single most important book you should read is *Capitalism and Freedom*, the classic statement of economic philosophy by that ever-provocative winner of the 1976 Nobel Prize in economics, Milton Friedman.

- Unemployment insurance
- Old-age insurance
- Universal health insurance

Today, of course, we have two of these three programs (unemployment insurance and old-age insurance, or Social Security, as we call it now). In fact, these two programs were really the backbone of what we now refer to as FDR's New Deal. Incidentally, this was also the beginning of what Republicans now call big government.

ENTITLEMENTS—PART II

FDR remained the man with the plan for a great number of years. (So long, in fact, that he's the only president who has ever served longer than two terms.)

Then, along came Lyndon Baines Johnson and his Great Society. As LBJ said in his 1965 State of the Union address:

> We worked for two centuries to climb this peak of prosperity. But we are only at the beginning of the road to the Great Society. Ahead now is a summit where freedom from the wants of the body can help fulfill the needs of the spirit. . . . The Great Society asks not how much, but how good; not only how to create wealth but how to use it; not only how fast we are going, but where we are headed.

As part of LBJ's vision of a "great society," he envisioned 60 separate bills that provided for new and better-equipped classrooms, scholarships for minorities, and low-interest student loans; the Medicare program, which guaranteed health care for every American over 65; environmental measures designed to reclaim polluted air and water; the National Foundation on the Arts and the Humanities; the Job Corps; and an educational program for underprivileged four- and five-year-old children called Head Start. Since Johnson was in office, the government has grown to include many

---

DON'T BELIEVE EVERYTHING YOU'RE TOLD

Never take the rhetoric, promises, predictions of a president too seriously. After all, it was Herbert Hoover who announced, in his speech accepting the Republican nomination for the presidency in 1928, that ". . . we in America today are nearer to the final triumph over poverty than ever before in the history of any land. The poorhouse is vanishing from among us. We have not yet reached the goal, but given a chance to go forward with the policies of the last eight years, we shall soon with the help of God be in sight of the day when poverty will be banished from this nation." Of course, less than a year later, the stock market crashed and the Great Depression soon followed.

other aid programs and agencies: student loans, food stamps, the Department of Housing and Urban Development, and so on. In fact, there is probably not a single citizen of the United States who doesn't directly benefit from at least one government program.

For what it's worth, consider the cost of entitlements from FDR to LBJ and beyond. In 1998, entitlements cost approximately $836 billion, or a little more than half of the U.S. budget. Shocking? Yes. Unheard of? No.

According to journalist George Will, the federal government has been doling out huge amounts of the budget for entitlements for a long, long time. In fact, as he points out in an essay he wrote in 1996, 42% of the federal budget in 1893 went toward entitlements for Civil War vets. (See graph on page 97.)

DEBT? OR DEFICIT? TWO OF THREE DOCTORS AREN'T REALLY SURE

Of course, we can't talk about government spending without also talking about the national debt. And the national deficit.

Have you ever noticed that when someone's grousing about some "wasteful" government program or another, they tend to use these two expressions—*the national debt* and *the national deficit*—interchangeably? As if they were the same thing?

But . . . they're not. Right? Or . . . you aren't too sure? Don't worry. We understand. It's a tough question, after all. In fact, it's so tough, two of the three doctors we talked to (and these doctors happen to be winners of the Nobel Prize) couldn't tell us the difference between the national debt and the national deficit, either.

Q: Can you tell us the difference between the national debt and the national deficit?

A: Can I explain the difference between them? Is this a test? I'm sure you understand the difference and I think it's fair to say I understand the difference, and I hope this is not a test. I don't really like tests.

—HOWARD M. TEMIN, PH.D., WINNER OF THE 1975
NOBEL PRIZE FOR MEDICINE

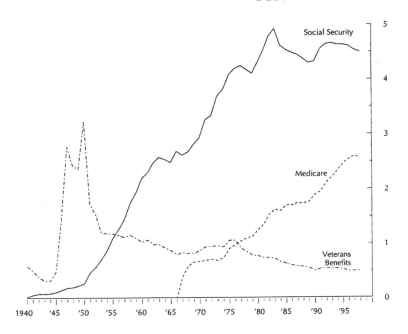

Income-related entitlements include unemployment, food stamps, housing assistance, retirement, and disability payments to employees of the federal government.

A: Debt and deficit? Gee, I would have to look it up in *Webster's*. *Deficit*, I think, means a negative balance, right? And that's to the best of my knowledge, but I can't be certain of that. *Debt* means "to somebody." The debtor owes money to someone—an individual or, in this case, the nation, right? So, I think it is somewhat semantic and they are often used interchangeably, to the best of my knowledge.

—KONRAD E. BLOCH, PH.D., WINNER OF THE 1964
NOBEL PRIZE FOR MEDICINE

A: Well, I guess the national debt is the accumulated deficits over many years. I assume a deficit is the amount of money that the nation has to provide for its expenses beyond its intake in taxes.

—ARTHUR KORNBERG, PH.D., WINNER OF THE 1959
NOBEL PRIZE FOR MEDICINE

Of course, Dr. Kornberg is exactly right. When you can't balance the budget for the year, you end up with a deficit. When you add up this year's deficit with all the deficits of past years, you end up with the national debt.

"HOW CAN I BE OUT OF MONEY WHEN I STILL HAVE SOME CHECKS?"

Just in case you're wondering how the U.S. government spends the remaining 47% of its annual budget* (see the info about the cost of entitlements in 1998, above):

- Defense: 19%
- Interest on the "national debt"†: 14%
- Other: 14%‡

WHY MISERY LOVES ECONOMISTS

In the world of economics, no news is good news.

We mean it. No matter what the latest economic statistic is, some expert somewhere will view it as good news. Another expert probably will view that same statistic as bad.

Although the release of these statistics may seem like random events to you—you flip on the radio and they're talking about unemployment figures or housing starts again—these statistics are in fact served up on such a regular schedule you can almost set your watch by them.

---

* These figures are from the 1994 budget. The fact that we say that should cause you to cock an eyebrow and ask: "But how often does Congress actually balance the budget?" Good question. And the answer is, they couldn't balance it even once in the years from 1969 to 1997 (and the last time the government balanced the budget before that was in 1960). And now it's time to lift your other eyebrow and ask: "So, if the figures above are for what Congress budgeted in 1994 but the budget wasn't balanced that year, how much did they actually spend?" Congratulations! Now you're thinking like an economist.

† The national debt, of course, isn't really just one debt. It is the accumulation of thousands of debts and the actual amount of money on the loan changes every day as some loans come due and new loans are made. Which raises the question: "Who is lending all this money to the U.S. government?" The answer might surprise you. The lenders range

THIS IS YOUR LIFE: AN AVERAGE MONTH IN THE LIFE OF THE U.S. ECONOMY

Business day 1: Nuthin'.

Business day 2: Nuthin'.

Business day 3: It's time for auto sales statistics, which are released every 10 days. You can tell a lot about the economy by looking at how many cars we buy. If car sales are up, that's good. However, if Americans are going too far into debt to buy them, that's bad.

Business day 4: Nuthin'.

Business day 5: Employment statistics . . . starring the latest unemployment figures! Lower unemployment is always good. Unless we're getting close to full employment—which is bad.

Business day 6: Nuthin'.

Business day 7: Report on consumer credit. Of course, when we borrow, it's good for the economy, for we are spending. However, it's bad for the economy because we're not saving more.

Business day 8: Wholesale producer prices. If they go up, that's good for the producers and good for the economy but bad for consumers and bad for the economy. On the other hand, if they go down, that's good for the consumer and good for the economy but bad for the producers and bad for the economy.

Business day 9: Retail sales. This is how much we the people spent on stuff last month. If we spent a lot, that's good—if you're a retailer or wholesaler. It's bad for us people, though, unless we're making more money this month

---

from people like you and us, in the form of treasury bills (or T-bills), savings bonds, and other lending instruments, to other lenders who are much larger and might even include the government itself. For instance, when the Social Security trust fund has excess cash, it might invest it in government securities because of the low risk involved.

‡ The category *other* for the government is sort of like the category *other* for you. The car breaks down, the roof leaks, you break your leg—who knows? There are some things for which you just can't budget. In the case of the government, these unexpected expenses might include funds to help cope with a natural disaster or an unexpected legal case (like Special Prosecutor Kenneth Starr's investigation into the activities of President Bill Clinton). The *other* category of the U.S. budget also includes certain agencies ranging from the Department of Transportation to the FBI to the Securities and Exchange Commission.

than we were last month. Of course, we don't know about that yet because the statistic on earnings hasn't been released yet. By the way, if we spent less last month, that's good, too, because it means prices have gone down and inflation is in check. Unless it means that we're broke and nervous about the economy and therefore hesitant to spend any money. If that's the case, then low retail sales is bad. Of course, it might be interesting to know what we're spending it on: More flowers for our loved ones would be good . . . more security alarms for our possessions because we're a frightened citizenry would be bad. But alas, this level of detail isn't reported on business day 9.

Business day 10: Inventory levels. How much supply do America's manufacturers and wholesalers and retailers have on hand? If they have a lot, that's good if Americans are in a spending mood. Otherwise, we'd suffer shortages. But if Americans aren't in a spending mood, high inventory is bad. It could lead to decreased production and layoffs.

Business day 11: Balance of foreign trade. Now, here's one you'd think you could always count on. If we're buying more foreign goods than we're selling, that's bad. That's what we call the foreign trade deficit and deficits are usually bad. Right? Well, not so fast. It might be that the reason for the imbalance is that the foreign economy has slowed. If so, then our buying their stuff means we're strong; moreover, it should help improve their economy and lead them back into being able to buy more of our stuff. And that would be good.

Business day 12: Daily double! Report on industrial production. This is just what it sounds like—how much product did our nation's factories and mines produce in the previous month? Report on capacity utilization: What percentage of potential output are our nation's factories actually producing? The higher these two statistics go, the better—that means more people are working. But if these numbers get too high, that's bad—too high an employment rate would cause inflation. (See **Business day 5.**)

Business day 13:	Consumer price index (CPI). See One CPI, Three GNPs, and 10 Quick Sketches of GDP on page 103.
Business day 14:	Housing starts. On the day they break ground, you've got yourself a housing start. Of course, when people buy houses, they set all sorts of economic wheels in motion. They get a loan. See **Business day 7**. Maybe they purchase new furniture. See **Business day 9**. And when people buy a house, it usually means they have a job. A good job. (Unless they're retired—see **Business day 5**.) So they can get the loan. On the house. And the furniture.
Business day 15:	Balance of the federal deficit. Unlike a lot of Nobel Prize–winning doctors, of course, you know what this is all about.
Business day 16:	Durable goods orders. A silly name, really, for stuff that hangs around for a while. You know, refrigerators, bicycles, washing machines. Sometimes, these are things you need for making other stuff, like pieces of machinery and tools and tractors. These orders are a sort of a measure of investor confidence (See days **10** and **12**), when you think about it.
Business day 17:	Nuthin'.
Business day 18:	Nuthin'.
Business day 19:	Gross domestic product (GDP). See One CPI, Three GNPs, and 10 Quick Sketches of GDP on page 103.
Business day 20:	Personal income. How much did we make, how much did we spend, how much did we save? See **Business day 3** and **Business day 9** above but not **Business day 14**.
Business day 21:	Nuthin'.
Business day 22:	Eleven leading economic indicators. Hey, it's the last business day of the month . . . what a great time to throw open the lid to Pandora's box. (See page 102)

PANDORA'S BOX; OR 11 LEADING ECONOMIC INDICATORS THAT'RE SURE TO KEEP YOU UP AT NIGHT

And on the twenty-second day, the economists give us chaos:

- **Average workweek:** Many of us with office jobs work 40 (or 60 or 80) hours a week because that's how the game is played. If you work in a factory or in manufacturing, though, the rules are different. You get paid for only the hours you work, and the number of hours they need you depends on how many orders there are to fill. Your life is an economic indicator because there's a direct correlation between the number of hours you work and the health of the company, the health of the economy, and demand for the product.

- **First-time claims for unemployment:** This one's a no-brainer.

- **New orders for consumer goods:** Not only does this indicator measure current consumer confidence but it also accurately predicts short-term future production.

- **Stock prices:** Think of the fluctuation of stock prices as a Pandora's box within a Pandora's box. When stock prices go down, for instance, it usually means lower corporate profits are expected. Meanwhile, lower stock prices also diminish the wealth of stockholders and cause them to reduce their spending. This, of course, leads to reduced production, and so on.

- **Orders for capital equipment/investment goods:** When business is good, you tend to want to plow your profits back into the business to use it to make even greater profits. When business is bad, however, the last thing you want to do is invest in your own company—after all, how would you know you were ever going to get your investment back?

- **Housing permits:** See **Business day 14** above.

- **Vendor contract performance:** What a funny inverse relationship. Normally, you hope vendors will deliver the goods in a timely manner; however, when economists are measuring the state of the economy, they consider tardiness to be a sign of a strong economy. After all, one sign that times are good is that manufacturers have more orders than they can fill . . . thus, your order arrives late.

- **Change in unfilled orders of durable goods:** Usually this indicator refers to orders canceled or quantities reduced before the manufacturer has had a chance to deliver. If there is no change, that means the economy is still humming along. If there is a high degree of change downward, you've got trouble, right there in River City.

- **Change in sensitive raw material prices:** When these prices drop, that usually means domestic output is about to drop. Why? Well, ask yourself why it is that prices generally drop. Usually, it's because you have a glut in supply or a drop in demand. Since these sensitive raw materials are scarce by definition, we know there can be no dramatic increase in supply, so the drop in price must be because of a decline in demand. And a decline in demand for raw materials—sensitive or not—is a precursor to a drop in production and output.

■ **Money supply:** When there is a drop in the supply of money, it usually means the gross domestic product (GDP; see below) is dropping as well, for, as we just learned, a drop in money supply means people are either saving more or paying off debt. But in either case, they're not spending, and it's spending that drives the GDP.

■ **Consumer confidence:** "And how are you feeling about the state of the economy today?" Surveys of private citizens are taken by nongovernment polling organizations. Of course, you could just stop wasting everyone's time and look at **Business day 3** (auto sales) above. You might also think you could gauge the same thing by looking at **Business day 14** (housing starts) above, but you'd be wrong. Housing starts, after all, really gives a measure of how people in real estate and home construction today think consumers will be feeling in about as many months as it takes to build a home. Auto sales, on the other hand, is a direct measure of how consumers are feeling right now, since there's no lag time between the purchase and the delivery of the goods.

ONE CPI, THREE GNPS, AND 10 QUICK SKETCHES OF GDP

The gross national product (GNP) is great for measuring the total income of a country's citizens, the gross domestic product (GDP) will help you measure economic activity within a country's borders, and the consumer price index (CPI) reminds you why you're broke all the time.

CONSUMER PRICE INDEX

Once in a while, in this era of bureau-speak, government actually calls a spade a spade instead of calling it "an implement designed for digging that has a flat, narrow iron blade rather like a shovel, which is shaped to press into the earth by foot, as well as a long handle equipped with grip at the top, for accomplishing soil-oriented proj-

ECONOMIC INDICATOR FUN

For soft-core reading, check out *The Atlas of Economic Indicators: A Visual Guide to Market Forces and the Federal Reserve* by W. Stansbury Carnes and Stephen D. Slifer. Written by a former and a current executive for Shearson Lehman Bros., the book uses graphics and diagrams to guide you to an understanding of what indicators reveal about overall economic performance and this performance's impact on investment markets. For hard-core reading, see Gale Research Inc.'s *Economic Indicators Handbook*. It discusses almost every economic indicator you can think of from inception to the present day. At a whopping 1,200 pages, *handbook* is a bit of a misnomer.

ects in such a manner as to restrict backward movement of the carriage during recoil."

Such is the case with the CPI. It is a monthly index of consumer prices, or a cost-of-living index. It's an average of the changes in price of a predetermined mix of goods from one month to the next. The CPI is considered a major indicator of inflation or deflation, and many wage increases are tied to it. Therefore, if the CPI goes up, you get a bigger cost-of-living salary adjustment. And that's good. Except that an increasing CPI also means there's also a good chance inflation will eat up all of your raise and more. And that's bad.

The CPI is a "market basket" of 300 particular goods and services—these items range from new cars to a half gallon of milk. The Bureau of Labor Statistics monitors the prices of these items by making periodic calls to more than 21,000 retail stores across the country.

When prices go up, the CPI goes up. When prices go down, the CPI goes down.

Actually, there are two different CPIs. The first is called the CPI-U. It represents the purchases of "all urban consumers," which make up 80% of the U.S. population. The other CPI is called the CPI-W and it represents the purchases of "urban wage earners and clerical workers," who make up 32% of the population. Hmmm. This adds up to 112%. But don't be too concerned about it. There is an obvious overlap of subjects in the two CPIs . . . and an obvious slight to folks in rural areas.

By the way, when you see the latest CPI statistics in the paper, what you are really reading about is the CPI-U. Meanwhile, some say that the methodology behind the CPI is flawed, that the index overstates inflation. Here are their chief complaints:

▪ **The CPI doesn't account for coupon clippers or people who shop for things only when they're on sale:** If it's your job at the Bureau of Labor Statistics in Washington, D.C. to track the cost of P205/65R15 92T Michelin tires at Montgomery Ward and you call for a price on tires every six months, you're not going to know that you could have gotten two for the price of one if you had just waited a week and then shown up at the counter with a coupon.

▪ **The CPI doesn't account for new-and-improved stuff:** When the price of an item goes up, the CPI always assumes it does so because of inflation. What the CPI doesn't account for are price increases due to product improvements or enhancements.

▪ **The CPI doesn't account for trends and fads:** Even die-hard beer drinkers in the U.S. heartland started drinking more wine (and less beer) after it was announced a few years ago that drinking a little red wine every day was good for your heart. But the CPI didn't know that. The CPI doesn't understand that we're all eating a lot less meat, too. Changes in buying patterns affect the usefulness of the CPI in two ways: first, as our buying patterns shift away from some of the 300 goods and services in the CPI's market basket, the results of the average become less and less reflective of reality. And second, the prices of the goods themselves may be affected by our changing buying patterns. After all, if demand for wine increases dramatically, for instance, the price is likely to go up, yet the CPI will see only the price increase, not the increase in demand.

GNP × 3

GNP is total output produced by U.S. land, labor, capital, and talent . . . whether that land, labor, capital, and talent are actually in the United States or not. In other words, GNP includes the output of U.S. citizens working in France, U.S. corporations manufacturing in Guatemala, and U.S. venture capitalists lending money to entrepreneurs in Russia.

It does not include output produced in the United States that is manufactured by a foreign company.

When considering GNP, it's important to keep in mind that product is factored into the GNP only as final goods or final services. This avoids the problem of double- (or triple- or quadruple-) counting an item as it is processed or manufactured from raw material into part of a final good.

An example of this might be a cotton shirt from your local Shirt-World. First, the shirt is a farmer's little puff of cotton out in the field. Then it is harvested with all the other puffs and sold to a wholesaler. The wholesaler bundles it with a bunch of cotton from other farmers and sells it in a larger lot to a textile mill. The textile mill turns it into cloth and sells it to a garment manufacturer, who turns it into the shirt you get at the ShirtWorld Outlet Center.

As you can see, it's important that the GNP include only the final sale of that puff of cotton as a shirt—otherwise, the market value of that shirt would be severely overstated because of the number of times it changed hands in other forms. Meanwhile, there are three ways to look at GNP:

- The product approach calculates GNP using the market value of all final goods and services produced in the given period.
- The expenditure approach calculates GNP as the total spending on final goods and services in the given period.
- The income approach calculates GNP by adding up all the revenue received by the producers of all the final goods and services produced in the given period.

Regardless of which approach you use, the bottom line figure for GNP is always the same—yet economists can look at GNP from these three different perspectives to get a more precise picture of the economy.

THE MANY FACES OF GDP

GDP is the total output produced within the boundaries of the United States, whether or not it is produced by U.S. labor, capital, and talent. Therefore, the U.S.-made cars of Toyota, which is itself a foreign company, are included in the GDP. The GDP is a useful statistic for two reasons. First, it allows you to gauge the health of the current economy. Second, it allows you to compare GDP trends of the past with the current GDP and make predictions about where the economy will go in the future. Here are some ways to look at GDP:

- Real GDP in 1900 was $100 billion. Real GDP in 1996 was $8 trillion. But this doesn't tell the whole story, of course, because it doesn't account for some other pretty important changes in the U.S. landscape over those 96 years. For instance:

- Population in 1900 was about 76 million. In 1996, it was about 267 million. Therefore, to truly compare GDP between the two years (or any two years), you should divide the GDP figures by population.

- Another way to look at GDP is by the number of people in the workforce contributing to it. In 1900, there were 2.7 million people in the labor pool. By 1980, that number had grown to 108 million. So, of course, GDP has grown by leaps and bounds. After all, there are many, many, many more of us contributing to it and many, many, many more of us making demands from it.

- What about levels of education and training? Surely this has an impact on the quality and quantity of goods a nation can produce. In 1900, only 6.4% of the workforce was educated beyond grade school. In 1980, more than 66% of the workforce had a high school diploma or better.

- Of course, transportation plays a giant role in productivity and manufacturing. In 1900, the United States could boast of 150,000 miles of well-surfaced roads. These roads were designed to accommodate vehicles traveling at speeds as high as 10 to 20 miles per hour. In 1980, the United States was home to more than 4 million miles of roads, many of which were designed to accommodate vehicles traveling as fast as 75 miles per hour.

- What if you wanted to dismantle the GDP and see what it was made of? Inside, you'd find four major parts. From largest to smallest, they are consumption expenditures, government purchases, gross private domestic investment, and net exports. Let's look at each of these parts separately:

■ *Consumption expenditures* is another way of saying *final goods.* It's the end of the line for any manufactured product, and the reason it is counted here and not before is to ensure that nothing that went into the final goods ends up getting counted twice. Consumption expenditures generally fall into three categories: durable goods, which is any product with a life expectancy of more than three years; nondurable goods; and services.

■ Government purchases are, as you might expect—clever you!—purchases made by the government. What you might not expect to learn here is that more than 20% of the GDP is for government purchases—and most of those purchases relate to defense, education, and roads.

■ Gross private domestic investments are generally purchases made by businesses. They fall into four categories:

   ■ Nonresidential structures like offices, warehouses or factories.

   ■ Producers' durables, which include items that are used in the course of business but are not bought to be resold: computers, cars, and even forks, knives, and spoons.

   ■ Increased inventory, which, unlike producers' durables, means items that are purchased explicitly to be resold.

   ■ Residential construction, which may seem like a consumer purchase until you realize that it first required a contractor to make the investment of time, money, and materials to build it.

■ To calculate net exports, find the difference between the amount of products and services we export and the amount we import. As you might have already suspected, these days our net exports go by another name: foreign trade deficit. We consistently buy more goods and services from other countries than we sell, and that has been the case in all but two years between 1959 and 1997. It is important to note, however, that a foreign trade deficit does not always mean things are bad here at home. After all, the balance of foreign trade is as dependent on the value of the dollar and other currencies as it is on how much stuff we are buying from other nations and how much stuff they are buying from us.

THE PASSOVER PRINCIPLE

"Why is this economy like no other economy?" and three other fundamental questions to ask about every market economy:

WHY IS THIS ECONOMY LIKE NO OTHER ECONOMY?

Could it be that this economy is different only because it is the one you are living through right now?

Every business cycle has four parts or phases—the peak, the contraction, the trough, and the expansion:

- The peak is the point at which GDP is at its highest. "But how will I know?" you ask. You won't know . . . until the peak has passed. At every high point of the business cycle, you'll always wonder if another, higher point is around the bend or if the time for the contraction has come.

- The contraction is the point at which production drops off and unemployment grows. Since the economy has passed its peak, things have to cool down. And by definition, if you're producing and selling less than you were before, there are fewer people employed. A note of caution, however: Just because the economy is in a contraction doesn't mean that the GDP stops growing; it just means the rate at which the GDP is growing is less than it was at the peak, and less and less each quarter.

- The trough is, in a sense, a negative image (but not a duplicate image) of the peak. It is the lowest point of the cycle, and you won't know you're there—just as you don't know you've passed the peak—until it has already passed you by. Meanwhile, unemployment will be high, production will be low, and the GDP will be limp.

- The expansion is like the first hint of spring after a long stormy winter. All is gloomy and depressing and gray when suddenly, there is a perceptible rise in GDP and a decrease in unemployment. People are regaining their confidence and begin spending again. Production increases. Employment increases. GDP increases. And the cycle begins all over again.

WILL THIS EVER END?

Economics is so much a good news–bad news sort of affair. The good news is that when the economy is experiencing a contraction or is mired in a trough, then yes, the current depressing state of things may soon come to an end. The bad news, though, is that when the economy is expanding or has reached its peak, when you're all giddy over all the money you're going to make, this fun and exciting state of things, too, will probably come to an end soon.

If there is one sure thing about economics, it is this: Things will change. And if things are good now, they may get even better, but eventually they will get worse. And if things are bad now, they may get worse first, but eventually they will get better.

WHAT IS A RECESSION?

The word *recession* gets thrown around a lot, yet few people really know what it means. Simply put, a recession is the point in a contraction at which the GDP declines for two successive quarters.

WHAT IS A DEPRESSION?

"I shall not today attempt further to define [it]; and perhaps I could never succeed in intelligibly doing so. But I know it when I see it" is how Supreme Court Justice Potter Stewart explained his ability to recognize obscenity in 1964, even though he was stymied when it came to penning an actual definition. We find ourselves taking the same position when we try to define *depression*. And we're not alone.

In fact, in an effort to garner some help with the task, we turned to two different college textbooks and a paperback economics dictionary.

To its credit, the paperback dictionary took a noble yet utterly ineffective stab: ". . . a phase of the business cycle characterized by a severe decline (slump) in the level of economic activity. Real output and investment are at low levels and there is a high rate of un-employment."* Duh.

The two textbooks had even less to say. One called a depression "the problem of a slowdown of the whole economic system"† and the other‡ offered no definition in the glossary and no entry for the word *depression* in the index.

Here's the point: If things get so bad that we reach a state of de-pression again, you won't have to ask if that's what is happening. You, and everyone around you, will be suffering as you (collectively) have never suffered before (unless you were around during the Great Depression of the 1930s). You'll know it can't get any worse.

And if you're lucky, you'll be right.

But you'll probably be wrong. And it will probably get worse.

We've all lived through at least one recession—for instance, we had one in 1991. But comparing a periodic recession to an economic depression is like comparing the sinking of your toy boat while you bathe in the tub to the sinking of the HMS *Titanic* and its 1,500 lost passengers and crew.

During a depression, every aspect of the economy goes into the tank; pro-duction plummets, wages fall, spend-ing evaporates, factories go idle. As things get worse, they can only get worse. The lower production goes, the less labor is needed. The less labor that is needed, the more unemployed peo-ple there are looking for work. The more unemployed people there are looking for work, the less em-ployers will have to pay them. The less employers pay their few em-ployees, the less those employees (or anyone else) have to spend. The less people have to spend, the less they buy. The less they buy, the less factories and owners will make. The less factories and own-ers make, the lower production goes. And so on.

> **"BUT DOCTOR, I DON'T FEEL DEPRESSED"**
>
> **Q:** How do you know when the economy is in recession?
>
> **A:** When your neighbor loses her job.
>
> **Q:** How do you know when the economy is in depression?
>
> **A:** When you lose your job.

---

* The *HarperCollins Dictionary of Economics*.

† *Economics: The Science of Common Sense,* by Elbert V. Bowden.

‡ Whattya think we are? A couple of troublemakers?

This is the nature of depression. It is a seemingly endless downward spiral.

Now let's cross our fingers, reflect on the wisdom of Justice Potter Stewart again, and hope that those of us who weren't around in the 1930s never have to see a depression so we never have to know it.

WEALTH 101

We all want wealth. But how many of us will know it when we see it?

If you've taken the time to read the bestseller *The Millionaire Next Door: The Surprising Secrets of America's Wealthy,* then you've probably already come to the conclusion that wealth is not what most people think it is. Sure, there are rich people who wear their wealth on their backs and their feet, under their butts when they drive, and everywhere else they can. But as Thomas J. Stanley and William D. Danko, authors of *The Millionaire Next Door,* have illustrated, most truly wealthy people live below their means—owning modest homes, driving modest cars, wearing reasonably priced clothes, and taking few vacations—whereas those who give the appearance of being wealthy by living the fast, flashy life are usually just living on borrowed funds and borrowed time.

So, just how wealthy are you?

Our Nobel Prize–winning friend Paul Samuelson once used a set of children's blocks to construct a picture of U.S. wealth distribution. If you used the blocks to build an income pyramid, he said, the highest point would reach far higher than the peak of the Eiffel Tower, yet most people would find themselves within just a few feet of the ground.

Why should I walk when I can hire someone to do it for me?
—BARBARA HUTTON, FAMOUS SOCIALITE, EXPLAINING WHY A
SERVANT CARRIED HER EVERYWHERE SHE WANTED TO GO

If an economist gets too much applause from the affluent, you should always be suspicious.
—JOHN KENNETH GALBRAITH, FAMOUS ECONOMIST

Pleasure is worth what you can pay for it.
—WILLIAM RANDOLPH HEARST, FAMOUS RICH GUY

WEALTH 101 ■ 113

REPORT ON "THE STOCK MARKET REPORT"

Given all we hear in the news about the Dow Jones indexes, Internet stocks, initial public offerings (IPOs), and mutual funds, many people instantly think of the stock market when they hear the word *economics*.

Ironically, however, not much more of a tie exists between the stock market and economics than between supermarkets (or any other industry) and economics.

Of course the stock market is governed by the same five rules of economics (the law of demand, the law of supply, the law of elasticity, the law of self-interest, and the law of economic reality*) that govern any other product or service offered in the marketplace. Yet, we think of the two as being intrinsically bound because the stock market is so much sexier than the poultry business or the car wash business. Why, watching the stock market on a daily basis has become a form of entertainment for many people. Ironically, while we watch the Dow go up and down, we marvel at the perceived value of Yahoo! and Amazon.com common stock and talk about the true value of America Online over dinner with friends, most of us have forgotten (that is, if we ever really knew) how the behind-the-scenes functioning of the stock market really works:

> For a firsthand account from Wall Street, see the number one bestseller *Liar's Poker: Rising Through the Wreckage on Wall Street,* by Michael Lewis. Tom Wolfe, who wrote *Bonfire of the Vanities,* described this autobiographical sketch of a young bond trader in the go-go 1980s stock market as ". . . the funniest book on Wall Street I've ever read." •

- It all starts with an IPO. You own a business that markets a good (like the Chia Pet) or a service (like poodle washing). But you need money to get it going or keep it going. Where will you get it?

- Easy. You sell shares of ownership in your company, wisely retaining the majority of the shares for yourself.

- In exchange for a prearranged amount of money, buyers can purchase one share of your business.

---

* In case you forgot.

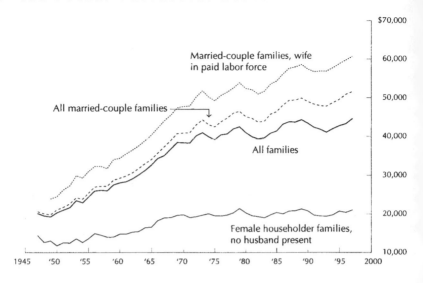

Ever wonder how you're doing as compared to your neighbors, friends, and relatives? Note: from the 1998 *Statistical Abstract*.

SOLVE THESE EQUATIONS

Apply some simple algebra to some trite phrases and clichés and you can reach a new understanding* of the secret to wealth and success:

■ Knowledge is power.

■ Time is money.

■ Power is work over time.

So, substituting algebraic equations for these timeworn bits of wisdom, we get the following:

$$K = P \quad (1)$$
$$T = M \quad (2)$$
$$P = \frac{W}{T} \quad (3)$$

Now, do a few simple substitutions:

Put *W/T* in for *P* in equation 1, which yields

$$K = \frac{W}{T} \quad (4)$$

Put *M* in for *T* into equation 4, which yields

$$K = \frac{W}{M} \quad (5)$$

Now we've got something. Expanding back into English, we get

$$Knowledge = \frac{Work}{Money}$$

What this *means* is that

- The more you know, the more work you do, *and*
- The more you know, the less money you make

Solving for *Money,* we get

$$M = \frac{W}{K} \quad (6)$$

or

$$Money = \frac{Work}{Knowledge}$$

From equation 6 we see that *Money* approaches infinity as *Knowledge* approaches zero, regardless of the *Work* done. What *this* means is that the more you make, the less you know.

Solving for *Work,* we get

$$W = M \times K \quad (7)$$

or

$$Work = Money \times Knowledge$$

From equation 7 we see that *Work* approaches zero as *Knowledge* approaches zero. What *this* means is that *The stupid rich do little or no work.*

———

* Author unknown; swiped from the Internet.

- But how big is that share? Logically, that depends on how many shares you divvy it up into. Think of your company as a pie. You can cut the pie into either eight slices or 80,000 slices. Now, if I buy one slice, I own either an eighth of your company or an 80,000th, depending on how many slices you've cut.

- As the owner of the company, you get all the proceeds of the initial sale of shares of stock. This is an IPO. Obviously, the number of shares is as important to you as it is to the shareholders. After all, suppose a share of your company sold for $10. If you sold eight shares, you'd get $80 (eight shares at $10 apiece). If you sold 80,000 shares, you'd get $800,000 (80,000 shares at $10 apiece). Of course, you don't get to directly decide how much each share goes for . . . that's the job of a market. And a market is evaluating the *overall* worth of your company, not the worth of each slice. Now, determining the worth of a company is not as simple as looking at the financial statement; it also depends on perceptions, expectations, and stuff like that. But to make the point about shares, let's say your company is worth $800,000. If you sold 80,000 shares, each one should sell for $10 because each one represents $1/80,000$ of the company. However, if the company was worth $800,000 and you sold only 8 shares, then each share should sell for $100,000, because each one represents $1/8$ of the company.

- Thus far, you'll notice, the stock market hasn't even come into play. What we've been discussing here is the IPO. The proceeds from the IPO go directly to the company's owners. But, usually, when you or I buy stock, we're not participating in an IPO. This is where most people severely misunderstand how the market works. Most people think that when they buy a share of GM or Apple Computer or Batesville Casket, the money they have just spent on the stock somehow filters its way back to the company. It doesn't. What you pay for a stock today goes to the owner of the stock. Which could be me or it could be Aunt Martha or it could be your mail carrier. Whatever dollars the company itself will earn from the sale of stock were already earned when the company initially sold the shares . . . unless the company sells more of its own holdings of shares or buys up shares and then resells them. So the company doesn't make or lose money directly when the stock price goes up or down. (Although the officers of the company remain responsible to the stockholders to run the company so as to maximize the investment shareholders have made into the company. And if the company does want to sell more of its shares, the price of the new shares—and therefore the money it can raise—will depend on the current stock market price.)

■ Although we rarely think of it this way, when we buy or sell a stock we are really buying or selling a piece of the company itself. For that reason, you could think of the stock market as a giant neighborhood yard sale. You don't want this bike anymore? Well, you own it, so it is therefore yours to sell. Just like your Intel stock. Meanwhile, you say to yourself, *I love the stuffed bear that neighbor Betty has for sale. I've got to have it!* "Will you take three dollars for it, Betty?" you ask. And either she agrees to your price or she doesn't. Fundamentally, the stock market works the same way. One day you wake up and say to yourself, *I've got to have some of that Disney stock.* So you go on-line to your Internet brokerage firm and pose this question (in the form of a bid) of everyone who has brought shares of Disney to the yard sale that day: "Will you take $32 for that?"

■ With all of this in mind, it is important to remember these key points when listening to the daily stock market report:

   ■ When a company makes an IPO of stock, it is doing so for only one reason: to fund expansion.

   ■ When you buy or sell stock, the actual company receives nothing from the transaction (unless you are buying or selling from the company itself).

   ■ The price of a company's stock on the stock market is based on perception of worth and anticipated future earnings, not on the actual amount you could get for the company if you were to sell it tomorrow. And the key word here is *perception*.

■ Let's say your friend Tony wants to open a pizza shop. You're a good friend, so you give him some money, in exchange for a piece of the action, so he can get started. Tony either will or won't run his pizza shop in a way that earns a lot of money. If he does, your cut of the action will far exceed your initial investment. And at some future time, you may even decide you want to sell that right to a piece of the action to someone else. So how will you determine a sales price? You will take a look at Tony's operation, you'll consider his track record thus far, speculate on how he'll do in the future, look at the neighborhood around his shop and try to second-guess whether it will grow and prosper or sink, and you'll try to outguess the competition. Then, on the basis of all that, you'll name a price at which you'd be willing to sell. Meanwhile, your prospective buyer will go through the same process to determine a price at which he or she would be willing to buy. And if you two meet, a deal will be made and a share of stock in Tony's pizzeria will get traded.

▪ Finally, it's important to say that although there is no direct link between the stock market and the economy, there are certainly lots of indirect links. For instance, when the stock market takes a dip, this may affect the perceived well-being of those who are in the market, who may cut back on their consumer spending. Simultaneously, companies whose stocks are on the downward swing may alter their spending, as well. And, of course, when spending decreases, the economy is affected. Additionally, it can be said that the stock market will usually fall before a recession and will usually rise before an economic expansion. This is why the performance of the stock market remains the basis for one of our 11 leading economic indicators.

BONDS. JAMES' BONDS.

At first glance, bonds are pretty simple things: they're corporate or government IOUs with a stated rate of interest that are payable on a previously determined day.

Easy, right?

When you buy the WXYZ Company's $1,000 20-year, 6% bond, you give them $1,000 today and they pay you $60 each year in interest and return your initial $1,000 (called the principal) at the end of the 20 years.

But that's just the beginning of the story, because it turns out that even though your $1,000 20-year, 6% WXYZ Company bond has a stated value and interest rate and won't pay off for 20 years, it can still be traded today just like a share of stock. It is precisely for this reason that bond trading leaves so many people confused.

Let's say you've got a 20-year, 6% WXYZ Company bond and you want to sell it. Well, how much is it worth? To answer that, you've got to consider:

- INTEREST RATE: The higher the stated interest rate, the higher the value of the bond. Of course your 20-year, 6% WXYZ Company bond is worth more than a 20-year WXYZ Company bond that pays only 3%.

- LENGTH OF TERM: The shorter the term, the higher the value of the bond. If my 20-year, 6% WXYZ Company bond pays off in 10 years, then it is obviously more valuable than your 20-year, 6% WXYZ Company bond that pays off in 15 years, since I won't have to wait as long as you will to get the principal back.

- STRENGTH OF THE COMPANY: If there is some doubt about the health of the company, then owning its bonds is a bit speculative. And as is generally the case in investing, when risk increases, so does the anticipated return. Given the successful 120-year history of the WXYZ Company, your bond is less volatile than a $1,000 20-year, 6% bond issued by your friend Tony who owns a pizzeria—therefore, you would expect to pay less for Tony's bond.

The final, and most confusing, part of bond trading is the way in which the bond's yield to maturity (or actual interest rate) is calculated. "What do you mean 'current yield'?" you ask. "I thought my $1,000 twenty-year, six percent WXYZ Company bond paid six percent." Yes, that's true. As long as you keep the bond, you will receive 6% on your money from WXYZ. But what would be the return to me be if I bought that bond from you today at a discount?

Before we answer this, you may find yourself asking, "Why would I be crazy enough to sell my bond for less than I paid for it?" The answer is yet another complicated aspect of bond trading. If the yield of your $1,000 20-year, 6% WXYZ Company bond is 6% and you realized you could sell the bond at a slight discount and then do something else with the cash to earn a higher rate of interest, wouldn't that be worth doing?

Meanwhile I, as the prospective buyer, am playing the same

game. I may have a bond that offers me a yield of 5% (because at the time I bought the bond, 5% was the going rate), and if I buy your bond at a discount, I will get a yield of 7%.

And now you are smack in the middle of typical bond-trading confusion: 5%, 6%, 7%, 9%—all this for a simple bond that promises to pay 6%?

To put an end to all this confusion, we offer this final piece of information: when you buy a bond at a discount, the interest rate or yield to maturity you receive will be higher than the rate of interest stated on the bond. And when you buy a bond at a premium (or pay more for the bond than the face value), the return (or interest) you receive is lower than the rate of interest stated on the bond.

So let's go back to your $1,000 20-year, 6% WXYZ Company bond. That was a good deal a few years ago, but the going rate on bonds today is 8%. So you sell your $1,000 bond at a discount (let's say $900). This allows the buyer to make more than 6% on your bond (since the buyer is getting 6% interest on $1,000 despite paying only $900.) Meanwhile, you can now use your $900 to buy someone else's bond at a discount and increase the rate of interest you receive. (Of course, in your case, when you buy that new bond at a discount you also have to factor in your already having lost money on your $1,000 20-year, 6% WXYZ Company bond when you sold it at a discount, but that's way too complicated for this book.)

Finally, you may be thinking to yourself: *I can see why someone would buy a bond for less than the face value, but why on earth would you want to pay more for a bond than the face value?*

Here's why: Let's say you still have your $1,000 20-year, 6% WXYZ Company bond. Only now, interest rates have dropped . . . significantly. Today, the going rate on bonds is only 3%. Suddenly, your bond is worth more than you paid for it, so if you decide to sell it, you can expect to get more for it than the face value. Always remember: When market interest rates go up, bond prices go down—and vice versa. Every single time.

And just when you think you understood the bond market . . . they throw new variations at you like the zero-coupon bond. Here's how it works: Instead of getting regular interest payments on your principal for the life of your bond, you buy the bond at a deep discount (we mean real deep, like $3 to $5 for each $100 of face value for a long-term bond), so that when you collect the face value of the bond at the end of its term, you are also collecting your accumulated interest for the years you held it. To put it more accurately, your income from a zero-coupon bond really comes from appreciation in value. Therefore, in some circumstances, such as for holdings within a retirement account—such as an individual retirement account (IRA), a zero-coupon bond can offer substantial tax benefits that a traditional bond cannot. Meanwhile, as with other bonds, you can always sell the bond at a discount or premium before it comes due.

THE POLLYANNA PRINCIPLE; OR, TEENAGE MUTANT MUTUAL FUNDS

It's hard to believe, but not that long ago, no one had ever heard of a mutual fund. Now they're everywhere.

In the beginning, mutual funds were designed to give average people a way to have diversified holdings and the skills of an expert portfolio manager at a low cost. In essence, the mutual fund took most of the work and a lot of the risk out of investing in the stock market.

That was then. Then was the early 1980s. There weren't many mutual funds to choose from, so choosing a mutual fund was pretty easy.

This is now: In the late 1990s, there were more than 7,500 mutual funds to choose from. Some offer remarkable track records. Most are average performers and do no better or worse than the market itself. Some are downright stinkers. Ironically, however, with this many mutual funds to choose from, it can be just as hard to pick a mutual fund as it is to pick a common stock.

Yet there has been another evolution in the world of mutual funds that has really caused some investors to sit up and take notice. It's called the socially screened fund and it works like this: You want to make a lot of money in the market but you don't want to profit from industries to which you are ideologically opposed. Maybe you don't want to own any mutual funds that invest in tobacco companies. Or in arms and defense contractors. Or in nuclear power. Or in companies that are known to freely pollute in the Third World. Or in companies that use sweatshop labor in Southeast Asia.

When you purchase shares in a socially screened mutual fund, you know the fund will never invest in certain types of companies. Therefore, if you are committed to withholding your investment dollars from tobacco companies or polluters or defense contractors, you can shop around for socially screened funds that have sworn off them as well.

It turns out that socially screened funds are good not only for the conscience but also for the pocketbook. Many are outperforming the market and earning healthy returns for their investors. Yet even when socially screened funds underperform traditional mutual funds, they are still a good investment for those who are environmentally or socially minded and who understand it is in their own best interest to make a little less (if that's the case) yet feel good about the fund they have invested in, rather than to make as much as they can at the expense of causes and issues they feel strongly about.

GETTING RICH AT WORK

Buying or selling slices of common stock from Tony's Pizzeria isn't the only way to make money. In fact, most people make money the old-fashioned way—they earn it by working hard. Just as in the stock market, however, perceptions can play an important role in how much you get paid. If you think you're worth more than you're getting, the smartest thing you can do is learn the right way to ask for a raise.

Of course, some jobs are best left to experts. For that reason, we sought out some advice from our friend Ed Brodow, author of *Negotiate with Confidence*, CEO of Ed Brodow Seminars, and negotiation expert extraordinaire.

HOW TO ASK FOR A RAISE

Here's Ed's advice:

1. **Do your research:** What's the company policy on salaries? What does it pay for your position? How much are others in the same job being paid? What do other companies pay for this position? And how important are you to the organization?

2. **Know what you want:** Don't negotiate for a salary without knowing what you want. Define your goals:

"Because that's where the money is!" said famed bank robber Willie Sutton when asked why he robbed banks. If you want a better understanding of where the money is and why it's there instead of in your pocket or in a deep hole in your backyard, see *The Economics of Money, Banking, and Financial Markets*, by Frederic S. Mishkin.

If the idea of following Willie's philosophy gives you the willies, see John C. Harrington's *Investing with Your Conscience: How to Achieve High Returns Using Socially Responsible Investing* instead. There will always be more recent and up-to-date books on the subject available, but this one lays out important principles in a comprehensive style.

How much will you take? What's the most you think the position will pay—and is that enough? Once you establish your bottom line, be prepared to walk if you can't get it.

3. **Think about benefits:** What will you take besides money? How about more vacation time, flexible hours, bigger title, more responsibility, stock options, pension plans, bigger office, and so on?

4. **Don't discuss salary as an afterthought:** "Oh, by the way, there's something else I'd like to discuss with you." Arrange a special meeting to talk about your salary and let your boss know that's why you want to meet. Give the subject the attention it deserves.

5. **Ask open-ended questions:** Be the interviewer, not the interviewee. You can accomplish this with open-ended questions— questions that can't be answered with a simple yes or no but that require some elaboration. Ask your question and shut up.

6. **Get your boss to make the first offer:** More open-ended questions. If you're interviewing for a job, ask, "How much does this position pay?" If you're negotiating for a raise, ask, "How much of a raise can you approve?"

7. **Offer an extreme position:** If the boss insists you name a figure, ask for more than you expect to get. After all, you may get it. If the bos counters with "The range for this job is X to Y," you can (a) go for the high end of the range or (b) challenge the range by explaining why you are an exception.

8. **Approach it from your boss's point of view:** Don't say, "I have nine kids and a big mortgage, so can I have a raise?" After all, we don't get compensated on the basis of need. Instead, remind the boss of the value you bring to him or her and the department and the company—and of the great impact you've had on the bottom line.

9. **Get your boss to affirm your worth:** As part of establishing your value to the organization, it's important to get the boss to validate that the company needs you. Ask questions that force the boss to talk about you in a positive way. Once you obtain this affirmation, his or her resistance will be lowered.

10. **Be prepared to walk:** I call this Brodow's Law—always be willing to walk away from a negotiation if you can't get what

you want. In a salary negotiation, your willingness to walk gives you tremendous power. The employer will sense it. Conversely, the boss will also sense if you are desperate and have no alternatives. Let's face it: The boss can't shoot you, so the worst thing that will happen if you walk is you'll have to look for another job—a *better* job. If you know what you want and stick to it, you will win no matter what happens.

"SURE . . . SAVE YOUR MONEY, SUCKER!"

If you're like most of us, you had parents who were constantly telling you to save your money when you were young.

Too bad they didn't know better, huh?

You see, although we are constantly bombarded with statistics about how little Americans save, what we rarely hear is how bad savings can be for the economy. And it's not hard to figure out why—after all, we live in an economy that revolves around stuff. And the only reason people who produce stuff do so is so they can sell it. And the only way they can sell it is if there is someone out there who is willing to buy it.

Of course, if you're saving money, you can't be buying, and if you're buying, you can't be saving. So if Americans save too much, that means they're not buying enough.

What if Americans aren't buying enough? Then the supply of money in circulation shrinks. Production drops. After all, why should producers produce as much when people aren't buying as much?

And when production drops, people get laid off. After all, if you're not going to produce as much, who needs all those employees? And what happens when employment drops? People without jobs have less money, so they buy less. People with jobs worry about their jobs, so they spend less, too. And when people spend less? Production drops even further. And so on.

All because your parents told you to save money.

OOPS! MAYBE YOUR PARENTS WERE RIGHT, AFTER ALL . . .

All right, let's cut the old folks some slack. After all, they didn't just tell you to save your money. They also told you to put it in the bank. (Today, they'd probably tell you to save your money and stick it in a mutual fund).

Guess what? They were right. In spite of the dismal picture of the effect of saving that we painted above, if Americans save money and invest those savings, then the outcome is good for the economy instead of bad.

It works like this: If you save $100 a month and stick it in the bank (or a mutual fund—the principle is much the same), then the bank has more money to lend. And who will borrow that money?

A. A business that will use the money to buy or create more inventory

or

B. A business that will use the money to invest in machinery or other capital goods, which will then enable the business to buy or create or sell more goods

or

C. An individual who will use the money to buy a good (like a boat or a car) or do something like add a room to his or her house.

As long as the money you spend remains in circulation (instead of being buried in the backyard or hidden in your mattress, for instance), then by definition it is money that is doing its part to keep the economy moving.

WHEN "GOODS" ARE BAD

Life is complicated. Far more complicated than in the days of Adam Smith and his "invisible hand." In Smith's time, all business was good business because all business kept money circulating and therefore kept people producing and eating.

Today, we recognize that not all business is good. The problem is, we don't all agree on what is bad.

Pick your poison: cigarettes, automatic weapons, violence on TV, porn on the Internet, pollution-spewing sport utility vehicles, land-devouring houses in the suburbs . . . Almost everyone has a beef about one of these products or services, including those who object to the rest of us who are eating beef and wearing leather. On the other hand, each of these "goods" has its own following of devoted fans who will fight to the death for their right to have it.

What all these purportedly harmful products and services have in common are their alleged externalities. In economics, an externality is the social cost of a product or service that is not included in the cost of production or purchase price.

Nowhere are the complexities of externalities more obvious than when the environment is involved. For example, while the local widget factory goes about its business of producing widgets, it also produces air pollution. Suddenly, 20 years after the widget factory relocated to your area, someone notes that the number of cases of emphysema has taken a dramatic rise. Is the increase in emphysema related to the widget factory's air-pollution output? Could be. If so, emphysema is an externality of local widget production.

When we talk about externalities, we are talking about economics at the extreme. Lung cancer and secondhand smoke are two externalities of the tobacco industry. But the industry itself is far too profitable and powerful to simply roll over and die. Instead, government tries to form regulations that will protect the rest of us (for instance, to protect nonsmokers from secondhand smoke, California has made it illegal to smoke in restaurants, bars, and most other public places) and push the costs of the externalities (like increased health-care costs) back onto the tobacco companies and their customers so the citizenry at large isn't stuck with the bill.

In the case of industry, one way government is dealing with environmental externalities is to sell pollution credits. Selling the right to pollute is one way government can limit the amount of pollution produced and also make industries foot the bill for the costs of their pollution. Coupling the cost of these high-priced pollution credits with stiff fines for polluting without them may make it cheaper for some manufacturers to reduce their impact on the environment by altering their production process; thus pollution is reduced further. (And in a final interesting twist, some environmental organizations are collecting monetary donations, using them to buy pollution credits . . . and retiring the credits before they can ever be used. Thus, in this creative way, pollution is reduced even further.)

AND DON'T THINK YOU'RE GETTING OFF THE HOOK

It's not just those evil tobacco companies and widget manufacturers who are guilty of polluting the environment with their externalities. You're doing it, too.

For example: Let's just say that as a consumer, you make the innocent choice to buy a house in the suburbs. The problem is that once enough people make the same innocent individual choice, society as a whole will suffer. Large amounts of land are cleared away to make a housing tract. This disturbs animals and plant life that make that land their home. Trees are removed that previously converted carbon dioxide into oxygen. Meanwhile, you and all your neighbors must travel longer distances to get to work. A highway must be built. More land and trees and animal life are destroyed or disturbed. Whereas most of you were once able to walk or take public transportation to work, now you each drive a car (except for the few who carpool). Because so many people have exercised their right to make individual choices, the highway is ridiculously crowded with traffic, and a new highway (and shopping centers and schools) must be built. Meanwhile, more and more people move to the suburbs and the cycle repeats itself over and over again.

Obviously we are not saying people who move to the suburbs are bad people. The individual's choice may be perfectly sound and the individual (like a couple of suburb-dwelling authors) may be very happy with the choice. But each individual choice has an externality, and each externality, multiplied over and over again may, in the end, be bad business for us all.

WHEN THE LAWS OF SCIENCE AND THE LAWS OF ECONOMICS COLLIDE

Written by scientist Rachel Carson, *Silent Spring* was instrumental in launching the environmental movement in the United States and worldwide. Reading this book will give great meaning to the truth that ultimately, economic laws must obey the laws of physics and biology.

". . . nothing less than an economic and cultural masterpiece, by the poet laureate of American capitalism" is how the editor in chief of *Inc.* magazine described Paul Hawken's *Ecology of Commerce: A Declaration of Sustainability.* Hawken is the cofounder of several businesses, including Smith & Hawken, Inc., and his book describes, in very meaningful and practical terms, economic issues related to the environment.

DECIPHERING ECONOMICS . . . ONCE AND FOR ALL

Early on in your economic education (or at least early on in this book) we suggested that economics is actually a fairly simple science, since it is, in the end, all about people just like us. We go to work, we make our daily dollar, we use it to buy some stuff, and in so doing we make the economy go.

Paradoxically, we've also spent a lot of time talking about government, big business, and big bucks—stuff most of us don't normally get to (or have to) deal with in the course of a day. Yet when you get down to it, the same five laws of economics (the law of demand, the law of supply, the law of scarcity, the law of elasticity, and the law of economic reality) apply. Much as you have to decide on the wisdom of spending $3 to get money from another bank's ATM, the federal government must decide whether it should spend another $3 billion to bail out another savings and loan and the American League must decide whether to enrage 3 million fans (and at least one Nobel Prize winner; see box below) by sticking by the designated-hitter rule.

BASEBALL, HOT DOGS, AND A NOBEL PRIZE

As a professional economist, I think baseball, of all games, has a capital value in maintaining the same rules, more or less, through time. All the statistics and everything are based on that, and if you change the structure of the game, you destroy the capital value. So I think it was very bad for the American League to put that [designated-hitter rule] in there.

Talking about baseball, there is one [other] thing I want to complain about. I think they have nearly destroyed the game by putting those goddamn big television screens out in the center field. . . . I'm sure it must affect the players too.

—JAMES M. BUCHANAN, WINNER OF THE 1986 NOBEL PRIZE FOR ECONOMICS

DO IT "THE COWBOY WAY"

Although a better understanding of economics may not make you any richer, it will undoubtedly make you a little wiser.

When most people (and businesses and governments) talk of

BIRDS DO IT, BEES DO IT . . . EVEN THE HEADS OF GIANT CORPORATIONS DO IT

Operate in a way to maximize their own self-interest, that is. Sometimes, though, businesses understand the way to make the most profit is to make a little less profit yet impress the customer by doing so. Alan Reder and the Social Venture Network delve into this phenomenon in the book *75 Best Business Practices for Socially Responsible Companies*. The Social Venture Network is made up of 500 highly successful, socially minded business leaders and entrepreneurs with a common goal: to integrate the elements of an ethically motivated workplace into a company's day-to-day operations. The book looks at innovative and creative practices of scores of successful companies, including 3M, Johnson & Johnson, Levi Strauss, Home Depot, DuPont, and Southwest Airlines.

---

economics, they talk of money as if—like love—it were a giant mysterious and unconquerable force without equal. From the Bible, which says "Love of money is the root of all evil" (1 Timothy 6:17), to George Bernard Shaw, who once wrote "Lack of money is the root of all evil," lots of people have had lots of opinions about money and economics. But we think it was Curly, from the movie *City Slickers*, who sums up economics—and life—best: "Do you know what the secret of life is? . . . [It's] just one thing. You stick to that and everything else don't mean s**t." And when Billy Crystal's character asks, "That's great. But what's the one thing?" Curly replies, "That's what you've got to figure out. . . ."

Thus, in seven short words, Curly explains clearly what hundreds of years of economists have not: It's your life, not economics, which is the big mystery. Figure your own life out—figure out where your own priorities lie—and you will have gone a long way toward figuring out your own personal economics and the economics of the world around you.

INDEX